AF694542

The U.S. Constitution and the Great Law of Peace:

A Comparison of Two Founding Documents

First Edition
Published by CIAC Press
(Center for Indigenous Arts & Cultures Press)

Copyright © 2004 by Gregory Schaaf
All rights reserved,
including the right of reproduction
in whole or in part in any form.

CENTER FOR INDIGENOUS ARTS & CULTURES
A division of Southwest Learning Centers, Inc.
A non-profit, educational organization, est. 1972
P. O. Box 8627
Santa Fe, NM 87504-8627
Phone: 505-473-5375
Fax: 505-424-1025
Email: Indianbooks@comcast.net
Website: www.usoriginalintent.org
www.Indianartbooks.com

Designed by Angie Yan Schaaf
Illustrations by John Kahionhes Fadden

Printed in United States

Schaaf, Gregory
The U.S. Constitution and the Great Law of Peace:
A Comparison of Two Founding Documents
p. cm.

1. United States History, Colonial, Revolutionary, Early National
2. Constitution, United States
3. Bill of Rights, United States
4. Iroquois, Culture
5. Iroquois, History
6. Indians of North America, Government Relations
7. Law, Constitutional
I. Schaaf, Gregory. II. Center for Indigenous Arts & Cultures. III. Title.

ISBN 0-9666948-2-1

The U.S. Constitution and the Great Law of Peace:

A Comparison of Two Founding Documents

Foreword by Chief Jake Swamp

Comparison by Gregory Schaaf, Ph.D.

CIAC Press

Santa Fe, New Mexico

Illustration by John Kahionhes Fadden

Benjamin Franklin learned that wampum belts
were woven as symbols of unity and peace.
Treaties united two or more nations, and the
wampum belts helped them to remember their promises.
Prayers were offered beneath the Tree of Peace.

Table of Contents

Illustration by John Kahionhes Fadden

The Haudenausaunee used wampum belts made of the quohog sea shell which was drilled into beads and strung into different patterns as a means of preserving history. The wampum belt concept was developed by Aiionwatha, one of the founders of the Confederacy.

Foreword

"The Roots of Democracy in America: Iroquois Influences on the U.S. Constitution"

By Chief Jake Swamp

The comparison of the U.S. Constitution and the Great Law of Peace is significant because it lays out clearly the similarities and differences between the two oldest founding documents in America. Our Iroquois chiefs and clan mothers have long said that the Great Law of Peace served as a model for the U.S. Constitution. We know that our ancestors met personally with Benjamin Franklin, Thomas Jefferson, James Madison and others involved in drafting the U.S. Constitution. This book provides documentary evidence to support the original teachings of our elders, recently acknowledged by the U.S. Congress that "the confederation of the original Thirteen Colonies into one republic was explicitly modeled upon the Iroquois Confederacy as were many of the democratic principles which were incorporated into the Constitution itself." (See Iroquois Confederacy of Nations, Senate Concurrent Resolution 76, S. Hrg. 100-610.)

The powerful story of the birth of democracy begins long, long ago. In the beginning, when our Creator made humans, everything needed to survive was provided. Our Creator asked only one thing: Never forget to appreciate the gifts of Mother Earth. Our people were instructed how to be grateful and how to survive.

But during a dark age in our history 1,000 years ago, humans no longer listened to the original instructions. Our Creator became sad, because there was so much crime, dishonesty, injustice and war.

So Creator sent a Peacemaker with a message to be righteous and just, and make a good future for our children seven generations to come. He called all warring people together and told them as long as there was killing there would be no peace of mind. There must be a concerted effort by humans for peace to prevail. Through logic, reasoning and spiritual means, he inspired the warriors to bury their weapons and planted atop a sacred Tree of Peace. He then established the Great Law of Peace uniting our original five nations. The Great Law was founded on democratic principles insuring personal freedoms and liberty, while establishing a three-part system with executive, legislative, and judicial branches of government. Benjamin Franklin called the Iroquois League a "remarkable confederation of nations."

Over two hundred years ago, the American revolutionaries dressed up as Mohawk Indians at the Boston Tea Party because we represented a model for liberty. They adopted the "Tree of Peace" and called it the "Tree of Liberty." The Continental Congress originally was called the "Grand Council" after the Iroquois Grand Council of fifty chiefs and clan mothers. A special room at Independence Hall was reserved for our Iroquois ambassadors. We were the first to recognize the United States as a new government. Our chiefs shared the Iroquoian model for democratic government with Benjamin Franklin, Thomas Jefferson, James Madison and other Americans.

This book provides a comparison of our Great Law of Peace and the U.S. Constitution compiled by Dr. Gregory Schaaf. I first met him over twenty years ago at a meeting of our Grand Council. He asked that we become his counselors in helping to prepare a speech to the United Nations. Our council became of "one mind" to support his request, and I became one of the chiefs who began to work with him. At the United Nations, the story of the Peacemaker was recounted, and we called for all the people of peace on Earth to plant Trees of Peace. We set our goal very high calling for one billion trees to be planted "to breath life back into the body of Mother Earth."

The message happily was well received. To help achieve our goal, we founded in 1982 the "Tree of Peace Society," a non-profit, educational organization. People from all walks of life responded from Dr. Robert Mueller, Assistant Secretary General of the United Nations, to representatives of almost a hundred world organizations. Tree of Peace planting ceremonies were organized at schools, places of religious worship and at State Capitols from New York to California. Trees of Peace were planted on the Mall in Washington, D.C.. Ceremonies were conducted from Ayers Rock in Australia to the foot of Mount Fuji in Japan. Over the past two decades, we estimate over 200 million trees have been planted around the world, but we still have 800 million to go. If you would like to join the Tree of Peace Society, request a Tree of Peace planting ceremony in your area, or receive educational materials, contact us:

The Tree of Peace Society
Mohawk Nation
via 326 Cook Road
Hogansburg, NY 13655
Phone: (518)358-2641
Fax: (518)358-9101
Email: treeofpeace@earthlink.net
Website: www.treeofpeacesociety.info

Introduction

From the time of the signing of the Declaration of Independence to the ratification of the U.S. Constitution, the opportunity to create and to establish a new government challenged people to search for the roots of democracy. One of the little known secrets of the Founding Fathers is the fact that they discovered a democratic model not in Great Britain, France, Italy, nor any of the so-called "cradles of civilization." Thomas Jefferson, Benjamin Franklin and others found among the American Indians the oldest participatory democracies on earth .[1]

Representatives of the U.S. Congress met privately with ambassadors from the Haudenausaunee, Six Nations Confederacy, as well as the Lenni Lenape, Grandfathers of the Algonquian family of nations. For centuries these American Indian people were governed by democratic principles. Through wampum diplomacy, their traditional philosophy of liberty was advanced in a series of peace talks focused on the law of the land, the balance of power and the rights of the people.[2]

American Indian Agent George Morgan and others served as intermediaries in these talks. His role as a diplomat demanded an intimate knowledge of the cultures, social structures and governments of the American Indians. He traveled safely through Indian communities and met with Indian leaders of frontier democracies. He witnessed societies where people were endowed with the right to speak freely, the right to assemble, religious freedom, as well as the separation of governmental powers into three branches.[3]

A system of checks and balances was firmly in place like the branches of the great "Tree of Peace" among the Haudenausaunee, "People of the Longhouse." The United States government was structured surprisingly similar to their Grand Council.[4]

SEATING PATTERN OF IROQUOIAN GRAND COUNCIL

CAYUGA	ONEIDA
YOUNGER BROTHERS (HOUSE OF REPRESENTATIVES)	
ONONDAGA FIRE KEEPERS (EXECUTIVE BRANCH)	WOMEN'S COUNCIL (JUDICIAL BRANCH)
ELDER BROTHERS (SENATE)	
MOHAWK	SENECA

The Onondaga, led by Tatadaho the Firekeeper at the heart of the Confederacy, paralleled the presidency of the executive branch. Their legislative branch was divided into two parts. The Mohawk and Seneca, united as Elder Brothers, formed the upper house of the traditional Senate. The Oneida and Cayuga, joined in 1710 by the Tuscarora, composed the Younger Brothers, similar to the House of Representatives.[5]

After meeting with representatives of the Six Nations in the summer of 1754, Benjamin Franklin first proposed the creation of a colonial Grand Council in the "Albany Plan of Union":

> One General Government may be formed in America . . . administered by a president General . . . and a Grand Council to be chosen by the representatives of the people of the several colonies . . .[6]

Franklin's plan for a Grand Council of United Colonies clearly resembled the Grand Council of the united Iroquois Six Nations.

Why did the Founding Fathers choose to keep secret the original design of the United States government? One clue may be related to a major difference between Iroquoian vs U.S. judicial branches. The Iroquoian Supreme Court was entrusted to the women. Clan Mothers and Women's Councils maintained a balance of power in their matrilineal society. Women nominated chief statesmen as political and religious leaders, lending a maternal insight into good leadership qualities. Their standards were set very high. While under the U.S. Constitution, qualifications of Congressmen were limited to age, citizenship and residency, Iroquoian women moreover required:

> All royaneh [Chief Statesmen] of the Five Nations must be honest in all things. They must not idle or gossip, but be men possessing those honorable qualities . . . Their hearts shall be full of peace and good will and their minds filled with a yearning for the welfare of the people of the Confederacy.[7]

Women also held the power to impeach any leader who failed -- after three warnings -- to serve the best interests of the people. If the Founding Fathers had disclosed the political powers of many Indian women, perhaps women like Abigail Adams, wife of future President John Adams, could have effectively assumed positions as "Founding Mothers." White women could have argued they deserved, at least, equal rights with American Indian women.

In behalf of the people, women preserved title to the land through families and clans. This may be another facet of the Iroquoian system that some Founding Fathers may have preferred not to make public. In contrast, women in the United States were not permitted the right to own land, nor even to vote, much less control over the system of justice. Iroquoian women also maintained a sort of veto power to stop wars. If women across the land had known the truth about the power of Indian women, the call for equal rights could have been heard earlier, and American history might have changed over the past two hundred years.[8]

Two generations ago, Dr. Paul Wallace, a respected ethnohistorian in Iroquoian and Algonquian studies, traced the The *White Roots of Peace* to the original sources relating how the first "United Nations" was born.[9] When I retraced these roots to Onondaga and then to Mohawk, I was impressed by a stone monument to Dr. Wallace which stands before the Akwesasne Mohawk Long House. On the top was engraved the Tree of Peace followed by these words:

TO AMERICAS OLDEST ALLY
THE IROQUOIS CONFEDERACY
"PEOPLE OF THE LONG HOUSE"
MOHAWKS ONEIDA, ONONDAGA, CAYUGAS,
SENECAS -- TO WHOM WERE LATER ADDED
THE TUSCARORAS CONSTITUTING
THE SIX NATIONS

FOUNDED BY DEGANAWIDAH AND HIAWATHA WHO PLANTED THE TREE OF PEACE AT ONONDAGA (SYRACUSE) SOMETIME BEFORE THE COMING OF COLUMBUS.

THEY EXCELLED IN STATESMANSHIP AND THE ART OF DIPLOMACY. AFTER THE WHITE MAN CAME, DURING MORE THAN A CENTURY OF INTER-COLONIAL STRIFE, THEY LOYALLY PROTECTED THE INFANT ENGLISH COLONIES, SHOWED THEM THE WAY TO UNION, AND SO HELPED PREPARE THE AMERICAN AND CANADIAN PEOPLE FOR NATIONHOOD.

IN MEMORY OF OUR BELOVED BROTHER
TO-RI-WA-WA-KON (DR. PAUL A. WALLACE)
WHO, THROUGH HIS WRITINGS, SHOWED THE
IROQUOIS CONFEDERACY AS IT TRULY EXISTED.
THANK YOU,
TORIWAWAKON, FOR YOUR GREAT WORK.[10]

Toriwawakon literally means, "He Holds the Matters," which implies that he held in his hands matters related to the core of Iroquoian society.

Dr. Wallace began the story by recognizing the Iroquois as the "famous Indian confederacy that provided a model for, and an incentive to, the transformation of the thirteen colonies into the United States of America."[11] Over a thousand years ago, according to Iroquois faith-keepers, a Great Peacemaker emerged at the time of a terrible war. He inspired the warriors to bury their weapons of war beneath a sacred Tree of Peace. An eagle soared from the heavens, perched on top of the tree and clutched the arrows to symbolize the united Indian nations. (The U.S. National Seal, pictured on the back of the one dollar bill, features 13 arrows for the 13 original United States.)[12]

The Haudenausaunee have preserved a story of the origins of the Tree of Peace. At the planting of a Tree of Peace at Philadelphia, Chief Swamp explained through interpreter Chief Tom Porter.[13]

Upon hearing this story, Dr. Robert Muller, former Assistant Secretary General of the United Nations, responded, "This profound action stands as perhaps the oldest effort for disarmament in world history."[14]

The Peacemaker provided the people with a code of justice called the Great Law of Peace.[15] His vision embraced all the people of the world joining hands in a way of life based on the principle that peace is the law of the land. He created a united government which still meets around the council fire at Onondaga, near present-day Syracuse, New York.

The rights of the people, according to Onondaga Faithkeeper Oren Lyons, include, "freedom of speech, freedom of religion, and the rights of women to participate in government. The concept of separation of powers in government and of checks and balances of power within governments are traceable to our constitution. These are ideas learned by the colonists."[16]

Over 200 years ago an Onondaga chief advised Benjamin Franklin and other colonial representatives, "Our wise Forefathers established Union and Amity. this made us formidable. We are a powerful Confederacy, and if you observe the same methods . . . you will acquire fresh Strength and Power."[17] Franklin challenged the colonists to create a similar united government:

> It would be a strange thing if (the) Six Nations . . . should be capable of forming . . . such a union . . . and yet a like union should be impracticable for . . . a dozen English colonies.[18]

The result of Franklin's challenge was the creation of the United States of America with a Bill of Rights and Constitution based on the Great Law as symbolized by the Tree of Peace.

The first U.S. - Indian peace treaty in 1776 took place beneath a Tree of Peace, as documented in the Morgan Papers, the documents of the American Indian agent who recorded how the elders tried to promote peace during the Revolutionary War.[19] In the spring of 1776, the Continental Congress decided to retrace the White Roots of Peace by appointing the first Indian Agent George Morgan to promote peace among the Indian nations.[20] John Hancock, the President of Congress, instructed Morgan to take a "great peace belt with 13 diamonds and 2,500 wampum beads," following the custom of the Peacemaker when inviting the Indians to attend the first U.S. - Indian Peace Treaty.[21] The details of the wampum diplomacy -- which featured the philosophical roots of the Great Law of Peace and the U.S. Constitution -- came to light with the discovery Morgan Papers.[22] Found in an old trunk in the attic of 94-year-old Susannah Morgan, the collection features original documents by George Washington, Thomas Jefferson, John Hancock and Morgan's private journal that prove the Iroquois Confederacy advocated peace and neutrality early in the Revolution. To symbolize the American promise that Indians would never be forced to fight in the wars of the U.S. and that Indian land rights would be respected, the American Indian Commissioners presented the chiefs and clan mothers with the 13 diamond wampum belt. Symbolically, the war hatchet was then buried beneath the Tree of Peace, and prayers of peace were offered through the sacred pipe.[23]

The Tree of Peace thus became the Tree of Liberty, and the Eagle atop clutched 13 arrows for the 13 states. While the Iroquois shared the Peacemakers plan for creating a strong united government which influenced the U.S. Constitution, Washington also wanted Iroquois men to fight in the war and Iroquois land for American expansion. The Six Nations were forced to take a stand for their own freedom and liberty.[24]

Based on the Great Law of Peace, the Peacemaker founded a participatory democracy in which the people have the right to actively participate and to determine their own future. The Iroquois Constitution laid the foundation for a government of the people with three branches. The democratic government of the Lenni Lenape, Grandfathers of the Algonquian family of nations, also guaranteed freedom of religion, freedom of speech, and right of assembly long before these rights were extended to American citizens.[25] As acknowledged in the writings of Benjamin Franklin, George Morgan and other founding fathers, frontier democracy clearly influenced the framers of the U.S. Constitution.

Iroquoian elders have long claimed their government served as a model for the United States. To put their tradition to a test, appropriate passages from the Great Law of Peace have been positioned side-by-side with the Constitution of the United States of America. The results proved striking. The parallels are unmistakable. Moreover, the differences proved even more interesting. Featuring high qualifications for leadership, political rights for women and a remarkable system of justice, the Great Law of Peace may inspire people to reconsider the founding principles of America's origins.

Footnotes

1. Two main schools of thought have dominated scholarly interpretation. The Imperial school looked east primarily to British institutions and French philosophy by Rousseau, Locke and others. The Frontier school led by Frederick Jackson Turner looked west to sectional influences. This study draws a focus on the influence of American Indians, particularly the Iroquoian and Algonquian nations known collectively and the Eastern Woodland cultures.
2. Transcripts of meetings between the U.S. and Indian ambassadors during the American Revolution were compiled by John P. Butler, *Index: The Papers of the Continental Congress: 1774-1789* (Washington, D.C., 1978), v. II.
3. George Morgan's eyewitness account of Indian Affairs during the American Revolution is the topic of a book by Gregory Schaaf, *Wampum Belts & Peace Trees* (1990).
4. The "Seating Chart" of the Grand Council is illustrated in Mike (Kanentakeron) Mitchell, Barbara (Kawenehe) Barnes, eds., et. al., Roy Buck, "The Great Law," *Traditional Teachings* (North American Indian Traveling College, Cornwall Island, Ont., 1984), p. 37. The chart was developed by the author to include the Women's Council. The late Onondaga historian, Lee Lyons, first explained the comparison with U.S. branches of government to the author.
5. For an introduction to the founding of the confederacy see the accounts compiled by Seneca scholar, Arthur C. Parker, *The Constitution of the Five Nations* or *the Iroquois Book of the Great Law*, (Albany, N.Y., April 1, 1916). No. 184, 175 pp. (hereafter cited Parker, Great Law)
6. Benjamin Franklin, "Albany Plan of Union," (Albany. N.Y., July 10, 1754),

Queen's State Paper Office; British Museum, London, "New York Papers," Bundle Kk, No. 20, edited by E. B. O'Callaghan, (Albany, N.Y., 1855), v. VI. pp. 853-92.

7. Seth Newhouse, Mohawk, edited by Albert Cusick, Onondaga - Tuscarora, "The Council of the Great Peace: The Great Binding Law, Gayanashagowa," Wampum 27, originally coded 45-XLV, Tree of the Long Leaves (TLL), printed in Parker, *Great Law*, p. 38.

8. The Women's suffrage movement finally succeeded in establishing the 19th Amendment to the U.S. Constitution, certified August 20, 1920, "The right of citizens of the United States to vote shall not be denied or abridged by the United States or by any State on account of sex. Congress shall have the power to enforce this article by appropriate legislation."

9. Paul Wallace, *The White Roots of Peace* (Philadelphia, 1946, reprinted by Chancy Press with prologue by John Mohawk and illustrated by Kahionhes, John Fadden, 1986). (hereafter cited Wallace, *White Roots*)

10. According to Mohawk Chief Jake Swamp, the monument was designed by Tehanetorens, Ray Fadden, the Mohawk senior historian who established the Six Nations Indian Museum, Onchiota, N.Y.

11. Wallace, *White Roots*, p.3.

12. Dr. Donald Grinde and Paula Underwood Spencer are two scholars presently researching parallels between the Great Law and the US. Constitution. They mentioned to the author that a document has been found in which Jefferson made notations regarding the symbolic origins of the bundle of arrows.

13. Chief Jake Swamp (translated by Chief Tom Porter), "The Origins of the Tree of Peace" (Friends Meeting Halt, Philadelphia, October, 1985), tape 1, side 1, transcribed by Mary Beth Miller.

14. Dr. Robert Muller, "A Vision of Peace," (1987).

15. There are six versions of the Great Law of Peace and the founding of the Iroquois Confederacy:

1. The Newhouse version gathered and prepared by Seth Newhouse, a Canadian Mohawk, and revised by Albert Cusick, a New York Onondaga/ Tuscarora. This version has been edited by Parker who explained his system of footnotes as follows: "The abbreviations after each law refer to the sections in the original code and their numbers. TLL, means Tree of the Long Leaves; EUC, Emblematical Union Compact, and LPW, Skanawila's Laws of Peace and War. The first number in Roman numerals refers to the original number of the law, the second number, in Arabic numerals, to the section number in the division of the law named by the abbreviation following."

2. The Chiefs' version, compiled by the chiefs of the Six Nations Council on the Six Nations Reserve, Ontario, 1900. This version appears in the "Traditional History of the Confederacy of the Six Nations," edited by Duncan C. Scott, Proceedings and Transactions of the Royal Society of Canada (Ottawa, 1911), v. 5.

3. The Gibson version, dictated in 1899 by Chief John Arthur Gibson of the Six Nations Reserve to the late J.N.B. Hewitt of the Smithsonian Institution, and revised by Chiefs Abraham Charles, John Buck, Sr., and Joshua Buck, from 1900 to 1914. This version, which was translated into English In 1941 by Dr. William N. Fenton, Bureau of American Ethnology,

Smithsonian Institution, with help of Chief Simeon Gibson.

4. The Wallace version, a compilation of the first three and presented as a narrative by Dr. Paul Wallace, *The White Roots of Peace* (Philadelphia, 1946).

5. The Buck version, by Roy Buck, Cayuga, narrated in Mohawk and translated to English by the North American Indian Traveling College Staff, "The Great Law," *Traditional Teachings* (North American Indian Traveling College, Cornwall Island, Ontario, Canada, 1984).

6. Mohawk version, a contemporary interpretation by John C. Mohawk, Doctoral Candidate at State University of New York at Buffalo and editor for seven years of *Akwesasne Notes.*

16. Oren Lyons, "Elders Circle Communiqué." (1986).

17. Cannasatego to Colonial Officials, Treaty of Lancaster, *Pennsylvania Colonial Archives.*

18. Benjamin Franklin, the author found this quotation in Wallace, *White Roots*, p. 3.

19. George Morgan, Private Journal (April - November, 1776), 73 pp., Morgan Papers doc. 8.

20. John Hancock to George Morgan (Philadelphia, Pa., April 19, 1776), doc. 2, Morgan Papers, 3 pp.

21. For an account of the origin of wampum see Michael Kanentakeron Mitchell, Mohawk, "The Birth of the Peacemaker," *Traditional Teachings* (North American Indian Traveling College, Cornwall Island, Ont., 1964). v. II, p. 22-28.

22. Louis Thompson, "Historian Gregory Schaaf Strikes a Mother Lode of History Among a Neighbor's Keepsakes," *People Magazine* (January 24, 1977), pp. 20-22.

23. U.S. officials promised Indian traders at the 1776 Peace Treaty that Indians would never be forced to fight in U.S. wars. This promise recently has been recalled over the issue of young Indian men being denied college scholarships for refusing to register for the draft.

24. General George Washington's lobbying efforts to sway a secret committee of Congress to allow him to recruit Indian soldiers are documented in the *Papers of the Continental Congress.*

U. S. CONSTITUTION

(In Convention, September 17, 1787)

[Preamble]
We the People of the United States, in order to form a more perfect union, establish Justice, insure domestic tranquility, provide for the common defense, promote the general welfare, and secure the blessings of liberty to ourselves and our posterity, do ordain and establish this Constitution for the United States of America.

ARTICLE. I.

[Legislative Department]

Section 1. [Congress]
All legislative powers herein granted shall be vested in a Congress of the United States, which shall consist of a Senate and House of Representatives.

GREAT LAW OF PEACE KAJANEREKOWA of the Haudenausaunee, Iroquois Confederacy (Founded by the Great Peacemaker, Time Immemorial)

Wampums 1,2,3. I am (the Peacemaker] . . . with the statesmen of the League of Five Nations, plant the Tree of Peace . . . Roots have spread out . . . their nature is Peace and Strength. We place at the top of the Tree of Peace an eagle . . . If he sees in the distance any danger threatening, he will at once warn the people of the League. If any man or any nation outside the Five Nations shall obey the laws of the Great Peace . . . they may trace back the roots to the Tree . . . [and] be welcomed to take shelter. The smoke of the Council Fire of the league shall ever ascend and pierce the sky so that other nations who may be allies may see the Council Fire of the Great Peace [the eternal flame of liberty at the Center of the United Nations].

Grand Council

Powers are Vested in the Elder brothers and Younger Brothers

Wampum 9. 1. All the business of the Five Nations Confederate Council shall be conducted by the combined bodies of the Confederate (Chief Statesmen]. First the question shall be passed upon by the Mohawk and Seneca (Chief Statesmen - the Elder Brothers], then it shall be discussed and passed by the Oneida and Cayuga [Chief Statesmen], who later added the Tuscarora, thus the Confederacy became the Six Nations]. (10-X, TLL).

U. S. CONSTITUTION

Section. 2. [House of Representatives]
[Election of Representatives]
Clause 1. The House of Representatives shall be composed of members chosen every second year by the people of the several States, and the electors in each State shall have the qualifications requisite for electors of the most numerous branch of the State legislature.

[Qualifications of Representatives]
Clause 2. No person shall be a Representative who shall not have attained to the age of twenty five years, and been seven years a citizen of the United States, and who shall not, when elected, be an inhabitant of that State in which he shall be chosen.

GREAT LAW OF PEACE

Grand Council
Selection of Chief Statesmen
Wampum 17. 1. The right of bestowing the title [of Chief Statesman] shall be hereditary in the family . . . the females of the family have the proprietary right to the [Chief Statesmanship] title for all time to come . . . (thus the women nominate the chiefs who hold office as long as the women judge him to be fulfilling his responsibilities.

Qualifications of Chief Statesmen
Wampum 27. All [Chief Statesmen] of the Five [Six] Nations Confederacy must be honest in all things . . . men possessing those honorable qualities that make true royaneh [chief statesmen, literally "noble leaders who walk in greatness"]. [There are no age limits, but statesmen with a family and are citizens of one of the Five, now Six Nations, with exception to the Pine Tree Chief. The clan mothers and women evaluate who is qualified to be a chief statesman.]
Wampum 53. When the Royanch women, holders of a [chief statesman] title, select one of their sons as a candidate, they shall select one who is trustworthy, of good character, of honest disposition, one who manages his own affairs, supports his own family, if any, and who has proven a faithful man to his Nation.

U. S. CONSTITUTION

[Apportionment of Representatives]

Clause 3. Representatives and direct taxes shall be apportioned among the several States which may be included within this Union, according to their respective numbers, which shall be determined by adding to the whole number of free persons, including those bound to service for a term of years, and excluding Indians not taxed, three-fifths of all other persons.

The actual enumeration shall be made within three years after the first meeting of the Congress of the United States, and within every subsequent term of ten years, in such manner as they shall by law direct. The number of Representatives shall not exceed one for every thirty thousand, but each State shall have at least one Representative; and until such enumeration shall be made, the State of New Hampshire shall be entitled to choose three, Massachusetts eight, Rhode-Island and Providence Plantations one, Connecticut five, New York six, New Jersey four, Pennsylvania eight, Delaware one, Maryland six, Virginia ten, North Carolina five, South Carolina five, and Georgia three. [The part of this Clause relating to the mode of apportionment of representatives among the several States has been affected by Section 2 of Amendment XIV.] Representatives shall be apportioned among the several States according to their respective numbers, counting the whole number of persons in each State, excluding Indians not taxed. But when the right to vote at any

GREAT LAW OF PEACE

Apportionment of Chief Statesmen

[The number of Chief Statesmen was set by the Peacemaker, not apportioned by population. No direct taxes existed. Slavery was illegal. The idea of some people being considered less than whole was foreign and never accepted. Note "Indians not taxed" were considered separate, a status still widely asserted and defended.]

"According to the great immutable law the Iroquois confederate council was to consist of fifty rodiyaner (civil chiefs) [or Chief Statesmen, literally "goodness, like the Creator"]" (Parker, p. 10):

Elder Brothers:

Onondaga [People of the Hill] - 14
Mohawk/Ka-nin-ke-a-ka [People of the Flint] - 9
Seneca [People of the Great Mountain]- 8

Younger Brothers:

Oneida [People of the Standing Stone]- 9
Cayuga [People of the Pipe] - 10
Tuscarora (People of the Shirt] joined ca. 1710 ----
Number of Chief Statesmen 50

[Tuscarora, Delaware, Saponi, Tutelo and Nanticoke speak through the Younger Brothers]

election for the choice of electors for President and Vice President of the United States, Representatives in Congress, the Executive and Judicial officers of a State, or the members of the Legislature thereof, is denied to any of the male inhabitants of such State, being twenty-one years of age, and citizens of the United States, or in any way abridged, except for participation in rebellion, or other crime, the basis of representation therein shall be reduced in the proportion which the number of such male citizens shall bear to the whole number of male citizens twenty-one years of age in such State.

[Vacancies]
Clause 4. When vacancies happen in the representation from any State, the executive authority thereof shall issue writs of election to fill such vacancies.

Vacancies
Wampum 19. When the [Chief Statesman] is deposed [or vacates position] the women shall notify the [Grand Council] through their [runner of their clan], and the [Grand Council] shall sanction the act. The women will then select another of their sons as a candidate and the [Chief Statesmen] shall elect him.

[Officers of the House - Speaker of the House]
Clause 5. The House of Representatives shall choose their Speaker and other officers;

Chiefs of the Grand Council -- Speaker of the Grand Council
Wampum 14. When the Council of the Five [Six] Nations [Chief Statesmen] convene, they shall appoint a speaker for the day. He shall be a [Chief Statesman] of either the Mohawk, Onondaga or Seneca Nation. The next day the Council shall appoint another speaker, but the first speaker may be reappointed if there is no objection, but a speaker's term shall not be regarded more than for the day.

U. S. CONSTITUTION	GREAT LAW OF PEACE
[Officers of the House - Impeachment] **Clause 5. (cont.)** and shall have the sole power of impeachment.	**Chiefs of the Grand Council -- Impeachment** **Wampum 19.** If at any time it shall be manifest that a [Chief Statesman] has not in mind the welfare of the people or disobeys the rules of this Great Law, the men or the women of the Confederacy, or both jointly, shall come to the Council and unbraid [unseat] the erring [Chief Statesman] through [a man who has no pity].
Section 3. [The Senate] **[Number of Senators]** **Clause 1.** The Senate of the United States shall be composed of two Senators from each State, chosen by the legislature thereof, for six Years; and each Senator shall have one vote. [Superseded by Amendment XVII.] [Proposed May 13, 1912; ratified April 8, 1913; certified May 31, 1913.]	**The Elder Brothers** **Number of Chief Statesmen** **Wampum 5.** The Council of the Mohawk shall be divided into three parties [each has 3 chiefs totalling 9 chiefs] The Council of the Seneca shall be divided into 4 parties [each has 2 chiefs totalling 8 chiefs].[Together, the Mohawk and Seneca parallel the Senate. The chiefs are chosen by the women and hold the position as long as they serve faithfully. Each has an equal voice, but decisions are formed by consensus.]
[Classification of Senators] **Clause 2.** Immediately after they shall be assembled in consequence of the first election, they shall be divided as equally as may be into three classes. The seats of the Senators of the first class shall be vacated at the expiration of the second year, of the second class at the expiration of the fourth year, and of the third class at the expiration of the sixth year, so that one-third may be chosen every second year; and if vacancies happen by resignation, or otherwise, during the recess of the legislature of any State, the exec-	**Clans and Consanguinity** **Wampum 42.** Among the Five Nations and their posterity there shall be the following original clans: Great Name Bearer, Ancient Name Bearer, Great Bear, Turtle, Painted Turtle, Standing Rock, Large Plover, Little Plover, Deer, Pigeon hawk, Eel, Ball,Opposite-Side-of-the-Hand. These clans distributed through their respective Nations, shall be the sole owners and holders of the soil of the country and in them it is vested as a birthright. (94-XI, EUC). **Wampum 44.** The lineal descent

utive thereof may make temporary appointments until the next meeting of the legislature, which shall then fill such vacancies. [modified by Amendment XVII]

of the people of the Five [Six] Nations shall run in the female line. Women shall be considered the progenitors of the Nation. They shall own the land and the soil. Men and women shall follow the status of the mother. (60-LX, TLL).

Wampum 45. The women heirs of the Confederate [Chief Statesman] titles shall be called Royaneh (Noble) for all time to come. (61-LXI, TLL).

Wampum 46. The women of the Forty Eight (now fifty) Royaneh families shall be the heirs of the Authorized Names for all time to come.

Wampum 35. Election of Pine Tree chiefs - Should any man of the Nation assist with special ability or show great interest in the affairs of the Nation, if he proves himself wise, honest and worthy of confidence, the Confederate [Chief Statesmen] may elect him to a seat with them and he may sit in the Confederate Council. He shall be proclaimed a Pine Tree sprung up for the Nation and be installed as such at the next assembly for the installation of the [Chief Statesmen]. (68-LXVIII, TLL).

[Qualification of Senators]

Clause 3. No person shall be a Senator who shall not have attained to the age of thirty years, and been nine years a citizen of the United States, and who shall not, when elected, be an inhabitant of that State for which he shall be chosen.

Qualifications of Chief Statesmen

Wampum 24. The [Chief Statesmen] of the Confederacy of the Five [Six] Nations shall be mentors of the people for all time. The thickness of their skin shall be seven spans -- which is to say that they shall be proof against anger, offensive actions and criticism.

Their hearts shall be full of peace and good will and their

minds filled with a yearning for the welfare of the people of the Confederacy. With endless patience they shall carry out their duty and their firmness shall be tempered with a tenderness for their people. Neither anger nor fury shall find lodgement in their minds and all their words and actions shall be marked by calm deliberation. (33-XXXIII, TLL).

Wampum 27. All [Chief Statesmen] of the Five Nations must be honest in all things. They must not idle or gossip, but be men possessing those honorable qualities that make true royanch. It shall be a serious wrong for anyone to lead a [Chief Statesman] into trivial affairs, for the people must ever hold their Lords high in estimation out of respect to their honorable positions. (45-XLV, TLL)

[President of Senate]
Clause 4. The Vice-President of the United States shall be President of the Senate, but shall have no vote, unless they be equally divided.

Speaker of the Grand Council
Wampum 14. When the Council of the Five [Six] Nations [Chief Statesmen] shall convene they shall appoint a speaker for the day. He shall be a [Chief Statesman] of either the Mohawk, Onondaga or Seneca Nation.

[Officer of Senate]
Clause 5. The Senate shall choose their other officers, and also a President pro tempore, in the absence of the Vice-President, or when he shall exercise the office of President of the United States.

Chief Statesmen of the Elder Brothers
Wampum 3. To you Adodarhoh, the Onondaga cousin [Chief Statesmen], I have entrusted the caretaking and the watching of the Five Nations Council Fire.

[Trial of Impeachment]
Clause 6: The Senate shall have the sole power to try all impeachments. When sitting for that purpose, they shall be on oath or

Trial of Impeachment
Wampum 19. If at any time it shall be manifest that a [Chief Statesman] has not in mind the welfare of the people or disobeys

affirmation. When the President of the United States is tried, the Chief Justice shall preside: and no person shall be convicted without the concurrence of two-thirds of the members present.

the rules of this Great Law, the men or the women of the Confederacy, or both jointly, shall come to the Council and upbraid the erring [Chief Statesman] through his War Chief. If the complaint of the people through the War Chief is not heeded the first time it shall be uttered again and then if no attention is given a third complaint and warning shall be given. If the [Chief Statesman] is still contumacious the matter shall go to the council of War Chiefs. (66-LXVI, TLL).

[Judgment on the Conviction of Impeachment]

Clause 7. Judgment in cases of impeachment shall not extend further than to removal from office, and disqualification to hold and enjoy any office of honor, trust or profit under the United States: but the party convicted shall nevertheless be liable and subject to indictment, trial, judgment and punishment, according to law.

Judgment on the Conviction of Impeachment

Wampum 19 (cont.). The War Chiefs shall then divest the erring [Chief Statesman] of his title by order of the women in whom the titleship is vested. When the [Chief Statesman] is deposed the women shall notify the Confederate [Chief Statesmen] through their War Chief, and the [Chief Statesmen] shall sanction the act. The women will then select another of their Sons as a candidate and the (Chief Statesmen] shall elect him. Then shall the chosen one be installed by the Installation Ceremony. (123-XLI, EUC), (Cf. 42-XLII).

When a [Chief Statesman] is to be deposed, his War Chief shall address him as follows: "So you, _______, disregard and set at naught the warnings of your women relatives. So you fling the warning over your shoulder to cast them behind you.

"Behold the brightness of the Sun and in the brightness of the Sun's light I depose you of your title and remove the sacred emblem of the [Chief Statesmanship] title. I remove from you brow the deer's antlers to the women whose heritage they are."

The War Chief shall now address the women of the deposed Lord and say:

"Mothers, as I have now deposed your [Chief Statesman], I now return to you the emblem and the title of [Chief Statesmanship], therefore repossess them."

Again addressing himself to the deposed [Chief Statesman] he shall say:

"As I have now deposed and discharged you so you are now no longer [Chief Statesman]. You shall now go your way alone, the rest of the people of the Confederacy will not go with you, for we know not the kind of mind that possesses you. As the Creator has nothing to do with wrong so he will not come to rescue you from the precipice of destruction in which you have cast yourself. You shall never be restored to the position which you once occupied."

Then shall the War Chief address himself to the [Chief Statesmen] of the Nation to which the deposed [Chief Statesman] belongs and say:

"Know you, my [Chief Statesmen], that I have taken the deer's antlers from the brow of ________, the emblem of his position and token of his greatness."

The [Chief Statesmen] of the Confederacy shall then have no other alternative than to sanction the discharge of the offending [Chief Statesman] (42-XLII, TLL).

U. S. CONSTITUTION

Section. 4. [Election of Members of Senators and Representatives -- Meetings of Congress]

[Election of Members of Congress]
Clause 1: The times, places and manner of holding elections for Senators and Representatives, shall be prescribed in each State by the legislature thereof; but the Congress may at any time by law make or alter such regulations, except as to the places of choosing Senators.
[See Amendment XX]

GREAT LAW OF PEACE

Election of Elder and Younger Brothers --Meetings of the Grand Council

Election of Members of the Grand Council
Wampum 54. When a [Chief Statesmanship] title becomes vacant through death or other cause, the Royanch women of the clan in which the title is hereditary shall hold a council and shall choose one from among their sons to fill the office made vacant. Such a candidate shall not be the father of any Confederate [Chief Statesman]. If the choice is unanimous the name is referred to the men relatives of the clan. If they should disapprove it shall be their duty to select a candidate from among their own number. If then the men and women are unable to decide which of the two candidates shall be named, then the matter shall be referred to the Confederate [Chief Statesmen] in the Clan. They shall decide which candidate shall be named. If the men and the women agree to a candidate, his name shall be referred to the sister clans for confirmation. If the sister clans confirm the choice, they shall refer their action so their Confederate [Chief Statesmen] who shall ratify the choice and present it to their cousin [Chief Statesmen], and if the cousin [Chief Statesmen] confirm the name then the candidate shall be installed by the proper ceremony for the conferring of [Chief Statesmanship] titles. (65-LXV, TLL).

U. S. CONSTITUTION	GREAT LAW OF PEACE
[Congress to Meet Annually] **Clause 2.** The Congress shall assemble at least once in every year, and such meeting shall be on the first Monday in December, unless they shall by law appoint a different day. [Changed to January 3rd by Amendment XX]	**Grand Council to Meet Whenever There is a Need** **Wampum 3.** When there is any business to be transacted and the Confederate Council is not in session, a messenger shall be dispatched either to Adodarho, Hononwirehtonh or Skanawatih. Fire Keepers, or to their War Chiefs with a full statement of the case desired to be considered. Then shall Adodarhoh call his cousin (associate) [Chief Statesmen] together and consider whether or not the case is of sufficient importance to demand the attention of the Confederate Council. If so, Adodarhoh shall dispatch messengers to summon all the Confederate [Chief Statesmen] together to assemble beneath the Tree of the Long Leaves . . . (4-IV, TLL).
Section. 5. [Power and Duties of Each House of Congress]	**Powers and Duties of Each Nation of the Grand Council**
[Sole Judge of Qualifications of Members] **Clause 1.** Each house shall be the judge of the elections, returns and qualifications of its own members, and a majority of each shall constitute a quorum to do business; but a smaller number may adjourn from day to day, and may be authorized to compel the attendance of absent members, in such manner, and under such penalties as each House may provide.	**Sole Judge of Qualifications of Members** **Wampum 17.** A bunch of a certain number of shell (wampum) strings each two spans in length shall be given to each of the female families in which the [Chief Statesmanship] titles are vested. The right of bestowing the title shall be hereditary in the family of females legally possessing the bunch of shell strings and the strings shall be the token that the females of the family have the proprietary right to the [Chief Statesmanship] title for all time to come, subject to certain restrictions hereinafter mentioned. (59-LIX, TLL). **Wampum 18.** If any Confederate [Chief Statesman] neglects or

refuses to attend the Confederate Council, the other [Chief Statesmen] of the Nation of which he is a member shall require their War Chief to request the female sponsors of the [Chief Statesman] so guilty of defection to demand his attendance of the Council. If he refuses, the women holding the title shall immediately select another candidate for the title.

No [Chief Statesman] shall be asked more than once to attend the Confederate Council. (30-XXX, TLL).

[Rules of Proceedings -- Punishment of Members]
Clause 2. Each house may determine the rules of its proceedings, punish its members for disorderly behaviour, and, with the concurrence of two-thirds, expel a member.

Rules of Proceedings -- Punishment of Chief Statesmen
Wampum 52. The Royaneh women, heirs of the [Chief Statesmanship] titles, shall it become necessary, correct and admonish the holders of their titles. Those only who attend the Council may do this and those who do not shall not object to what has been said nor strive to undo the action. (63-LXIII, TLL).

[Journals]
Clause 3. Each house shall keep a journal of its proceedings, and from time to time publish the same, excepting such parts as may in their judgment require secrecy; and the yeas and nays of the members of either house on any question shall, at the desire of one-fifth of those present, be entered on the journal.

Wampum Records
Wampum 23. Any [Chief Statesman] of the Five [Six] Nations Confederacy may construct shell strings (or wampum belts) of any size or length as pledges or records of matters of national or international importance.

When it is necessary to dispatch a shell string by a War Chief or other messenger as the token of a summons, the messenger shall recite the contents of the string to the party to whom it is sent. That party shall repeat the message and return the shell string and if there has been a summons he shall make ready for the journey.

Any of the people of the Five [Six] Nations may use shells (or wampum) as the record of a pledge, contract or an agreement entered into and the same shall be binding as soon as shell strings shall have been exchanged by both parties. (32-XXXII, TLL).

[Adjournment]
Clause 4. Neither house, during the session of Congress, shall, without the consent of the other, adjourn for more than three days, nor to any other place than that in which the two Houses shall be sitting.

Adjournment
Wampum 8. The Firekeepers shall formally open and close all councils of the Confederate [Chief Statesmen].

Section. 6. [Compensation, Privileges and Disabilities, of Seniors and Representatives

Compensation, Privileges and Disabilities, of Chief Statesmen

[Compensation -- Privileges]
Clause 1. The Senators and Representatives shall receive a compensation for their services, to be ascertained by law, and paid out of the Treasury of the United States. They shall in all cases, except treason, felony and breach of the peace, be privileged from arrest during their attendance at the session of their respective Houses, and in going to and returning from the same; and for any speech or debate in either House, they shall not be questioned in any other place.

Compensation -- Privileges
[Chief Statesmen do not receive monetary compensation for their services.]
[Chief Statesmen are not above the law in any case.]
Wampum 98. If either a nephew or a niece see an irregularity in the performance of the functions of the Great Peace and its laws, in the Confederate Council or in the conferring of [Chief Statesmanship] titles in an improper way through their War Chief they may demand that such actions become subject to correction and that the matter conform to the ways prescribed by the laws of the Great Peace. (67-LXVII, TLL).

[Disability to Hold Other Offices]
Clause 2. No Senator or Representative shall, during the time for which he was elected, be appointed to any civil office under the authority of the United

Disability to Hold Other Offices
[Although Chief Statesmen may not be appointed to any official office outside of his national duties, they do also serve as a spiritual leaders]

U. S. CONSTITUTION

States, which shall have been created, or the emoluments whereof shall have been increased during such time; and no person holding any office under the United States, shall be a member of either House during his continuance in office. [See also Section 3 of the Fourteen Amendment]

GREAT LAW OF PEACE

Wampum 26. It shall be the duty of all the Five [Six] Nations Confederate [Chief Statesmen], from time to time as occasion demands, to act as mentors and spiritual guides of their people and remind them of their Creator's will and words. They shall say:

"Hearken, that peace may continue unto future days!

"Always listen to the words of the Great Creator, for he has spoken.

"United People, let not evil find lodging in your minds.

"For the Great Creator has spoken and the cause of Peace shall not become old.

"The cause of peace shall not die if you remember the Great Creator."

Every Confederate [Chief Statesman] shall speak words such as these to promote peace. (37-XXXVII, TLL).

U. S. CONSTITUTION

Section. 7. [Mode of Passing Laws]

[Special Provision as the Revenue Laws]

Clause 1. All bills for raising revenue shall originate in the House of Representatives; but the Senate may propose or concur with amendments as on other bills.

GREAT LAW OF PEACE

Mode of Passing Laws

No Special Provision as the Revenue Laws

U. S. CONSTITUTION

[Laws, How Enacted]

Clause 2. Every bill which shall have passed the House of Representatives and the Senate, shall, before it become a law, be presented to the President of the United States; If he approve he shall sign it, but if not he shall return it, with his objections to that House in which it shall have originated, who shall enter the

GREAT LAW OF PEACE

Decisions, How Enacted

Wampum 9. All the business of the Five [Six] Nations Confederate Council shall be conducted by the two combined bodies of Confederate [Chief Statesmen]. First the question shall be passed upon by the Mohawk and Seneca [Elder Brothers] [Chief Statesmen], then it shall be discussed and passed by the Oneida and

U. S. CONSTITUTION	GREAT LAW OF PEACE
objections at large on their journal, and proceed to reconsider it. If after such reconsideration two-thirds of that House shall agree to pass the bill, it shall be sent, together with the objections, to the other House, by which it shall likewise be reconsidered, and if approved by two-thirds of that House, it shall become a law. But in all such cases the votes of both Houses shall be determined by yeas and nays, and the names of the persons voting for and against the bill shall be entered on the journal of each House respectively. If any bill shall not be returned by the President within ten days (Sundays excepted) after it shall have been presented to him, the same shall be a law, in like manner as if he had signed it, unless the Congress by their adjournment prevent its return, in which case it shall not be a law.	Cayuga [Younger Brothers] [Chief Statesmen]. Their decisions shall then be referred to the Onondaga [Chief Statesmen], (Fire Keepers) for final judgment. (10-XI, TLL). **Wampum 10**. In all cases the procedure must be as follows: when the Mohawk and Seneca [Chief Statesmen] have unanimously agreed upon a question, they shall report their decision to the Cayuga and Oneida [Chief Statesmen] who shall deliberate upon the question and report a unanimous decision to the Mohawk [Chief Statesmen]. The Mohawk [Chief Statesmen] will then report the standing of the case to the Firekeepers [Onondaga], who shall render a decision (17-XVII, TLL) as they see fit in case of a disagreement by the two bodies, or confirm the decisions of the two bodies if they are identical. The Fire Keepers shall then report their decision to the Mohawk [Chief Statesmen] who shall announce it to the open council. (12-XII, TLL).
[Resolutions, Etc.] **Clause 3.** Every order, resolution, or vote to which the concurrence of the Senate and House of Representatives may be necessary (except on a question of adjournment) shall be presented to the President of the United States; and before the same shall take effect, shall be approved by him, or being disapproved by him, shall be repassed by two-thirds of the Senate and House of Representatives, according to the rules and limitations prescribed	**Decisions, Etc.** **Wampum 12.** When a case comes before the Onondaga [Chief Statesmen] (Fire Keepers) for discussion and decision. Adodarho shall introduce the matter to his [fellow Chief Statesmen] who shall then discuss it in their two bodies. Every Onondaga [Chief Statesman] except Hononwiretonh shall deliberate and he shall listen only. When a unanimous decision shall have been reached by the two bodies of Fire Keepers, Adodarho shall notify Hononwiretonh of

in the case of a bill.

Section. 8.
[Powers Granted to Congress]

[Taxation]
Clause 1. The Congress shall have power to lay and collect taxes, duties, imposts and excises, to pay the debts and provide for the common defense and general welfare of the United States; but all duties, imposts and excises shall be uniform throughout the United States;

[Loans]
Clause 2. To borrow money on the credit of the United States;

[Commerce]
Clause 3. To regulate commerce with foreign nations, and among the several States, and with the Indian tribes;

[Naturalization and Bankruptcies]
Clause 4. To establish an uniform rule of naturalization, and uniform laws on the subject of

the fact when he shall confirm it. He shall refuse to confirm a decision if it is not unanimously agreed upon by both sides of the Fire Keepers. (19-XIX, TLL).
Wampum 11. If through any misunderstanding or obstinacy on the part of the Fire Keepers, they render a decision at variance with that of the Two Sides, the Two Sides shall reconsider the matter and if their decisions are jointly the same as before they shall report to the Fire Keepers who are then compelled to confirm their joint decision. (18-XVlll, TLL).

Powers Granted to the Grand Council

No Taxation
[There is no taxation under the Great Law. There also was no money. Today, when there is a need to provide for the general welfare, the people who wish to help come together to work for the common good.]

No Loans
[There is no national debt, because there is no provision for loans.]

Commerce
[The people are free to trade as they wish, as long as they do not endanger the health and welfare of the people.]

Naturalization and No Bankruptcies
Wampum 2. Roots have spread out from the Tree of the Great Peace, one to the north, one to the

bankruptcies throughout the United States;

east, one to the south and one to the west. The name of these roots is The Great White Roots and their nature is Peace and Strength.

If any man [or woman] or any nation outside the Five Nations shall obey the laws of the Great Peace and make known their disposition to the [Chief Statesmen[of the Confederacy, they may trace the Roots of the Tree and if their minds are clean and they are obedient and promise to obey the wishes of the Confederate Council, they shall be welcomed to take shelter beneath the Tree of the Long Leaves.

[Coins]
Clause 5. To coin money, regulate the value thereof, and of foreign coin, and fix the standard of weights and measures;

No Coins

[Counterfeiting]
Clause 6. To provide for the punishment of counterfeiting the securities and current coin of the United States;

No Counterfeiting
[However, Europeans made and distributed counterfeit wampum which disrupted the economy.]

[Post Office]
Clause 7. To establish post offices and post roads;

Runners as Messengers
Wampum 40. When the [Chief Statesmen] of the Confederacy take occasion to dispatch a messenger in behalf of the Confederate Council, they shall wrap up any matter they may send and instruct the messenger to remember his errand, to turn not aside but to proceed faithfully to his destination and deliver his message according to every instruction. (57-XLVII, TLL).

U. S. CONSTITUTION	GREAT LAW OF PEACE
[Patents and Copyrights] **Clause 8.** To promote the progress of science and useful arts, by securing for limited times to authors and inventors the exclusive right to their respective writings and discoveries;	**No Patents and Copyrights**
[Courts] **Clause 9.** To constitute tribunals inferior to the Supreme Court;	**Council Fires** **Wampum 96.** All the Clan council fires of a nation or of the Five [Six] Nations may unite into one general council fire, or delegates from all the council fires may be appointed to unite in a general council for discussing the interests of the people.
[Piracies] **Clause 10.** To define and punish piracies and felonies committed on the high seas, and offenses against the law of nations;	**Piracies** [The Great Law applies equally on land and sea.]
[War] **Clause 11.** To declare war, grant letters of marque and reprisal, and make rules concerning captures on land and water;	**War** **Wampum 80.** When the Confederate Council of the [Six] Five Nations has for its object the establishment of the Great Peace among the people of an outside nation and that nation refuses to accept the Great Peace, then by such refusal they bring a declaration of war upon themselves from the Five Nations. Then shall the Five [Six] Nations seek to establish the Great Peace by a conquest of the rebellious nation. (II-71, SPW).
[Army] **Clause 12.** To raise and support armies, but no appropriation of money to that use shall be for a longer term than two years;	**No Standing Army or Navy** **Wampum 81.** When the men of the Five [Six] Nations, now called forth to become warriors, are ready for battle with an obstinate opposing nation that has refused to accept the Great

U. S. CONSTITUTION	GREAT LAW OF PEACE
[Navy] **Clause 13.** To provide and maintain a navy;	Peace, then one of the five War Chiefs shall be chosen by the warriors of the Five [Six] Nations to lead the army into battle.
[Military and Naval Rules] **Clause 14.** To make rules for the government and regulation of the land and naval forces;	**Rights and Powers of War** **Wampum 81 (cont.).** It shall be the duty of the War Chief so chosen to come before his warriors and address them. His aim shall be to impress upon them the necessity of good behavior and strict obedience to all the commands of the War Chiefs. He shall deliver an oration exhorting them with great zeal to be brave and courageous and never to be guilty of cowardice. At the conclusion of his Oration he shall march forward and commence the War Song and he shall sing: Now I am greatly surprised And, therefore, I shall use it, -- The power of my War Song. I am of the Five Nations And I shall make supplication To the Almighty Creator. He has furnished this army. My warriors shall be mighty In the strength of the Creator Between him and my song they are For it was he who gave the song This war song that I sing! (72-III, SPW).
[Militias, Calling Forth] **Clause 15.** To provide for calling forth the militia to execute the laws of the Union, suppress insurrections and repel invasions;	**The Black Wampum Belt** **Wampum 91.** A certain wampum belt of black beads shall be the emblem of the authority of the Five [Six] War Chiefs to take up the weapons of war and with their men to resist invasion. This shall be called a war in defense of the territory. (83-XIV, SPW).

U. S. CONSTITUTION	GREAT LAW OF PEACE
[Militia, Organizing & Arming] **Clause 16.** To provide for organizing, arming, and disciplining, the militia, and for governing such part of them as may be employed in the service of the United States, reserving to the States respectively, the appointment of the officers, and the authority of training the militia according to the discipline prescribed by Congress;	**War Chiefs, Names, Duties and Rights** **Wampum 37.** There shall be one War Chief for each Nation and their duties shall be to carry messages for their [Chief Statesmen] and so take up the arms of war in case of emergency. They shall not participate in the proceedings of the Confederate Council but shall watch its progress and in case of an erroneous action by a Chief Statesman they shall receive the complaints of the people and convey the warnings of the women to him. The people who wish to convey messages to the Lords in the Confederate Council shall do so through the War Chief of their Nation. It shall ever be his duty to lay the cases, questions and propositions of the people before the Confederate Council. (54-LIV, TLL).
[Federal District and Other Places] **Clause 17.** To exercise exclusive legislation in all cases whatsoever, over such district (not exceeding ten miles square) as may, by cession of particular States, and the acceptance of Congress, become the seat of the government of the United States, and to exercise like authority over all places purchased by the consent of the Legislature of the State in which the same shall be, for the erection of forts, magazines, arsenals, dock-yards, and other needful buildings; -- and	**Council Fire of the Confederacy, Center of the Six Nations** **Wampum1**. I plant [the Tree of the Great Peace] in your territory, Adodarho, and the Ononlaga Nation, to the territory of you who are Firekeepers. I name the tree the Tree of the Great Long Leaves. Under the shade of this Tree of Great Peace we spread the soft white feathery down of the glove thistle as seats for you, Adodarho, and your cousin [Chief Statesmen]. We place you upon those seats, spread soft with the feathery down of the globe thistle, there beneath the shade of the spreading branches of the Tree of Peace. There shall you sit and watch the Council Fire of the Confederacy of the Five [Six] Nations,

and all the affairs of the Five [Six] Nations shall be transacted before you, Adodarhoh, and your cousin [Chief Statesmen], by the Confederate [Chief Statesmen] of the Five [Six] Nations. [1-I, TLL].

[Make Laws to Carry Out Foregoing Powers]
Clause 18. To make all laws which shall be necessary and proper for carrying into execution the foregoing powers, and all other powers vested by this Constitution in the Government of the United States, or in any department or officer thereof. [For other powers, see Article II, Section 1; Article III, Sections 2 and 3; Article IV, Sections 1-3; Article V; and Amendments XII-XVI and XIX-XXI.]

Adding to the Rafters
Wampum 16. If the conditions which shall arise at any future time call for an addition to or change of this law the case shall be carefully considered and if a new beam seems necessary or beneficial, the proposed change shall be voted upon and if adopted it shall be called, "Added to the Rafters." (48-XLVII, TLL).

Section. 9 [Limitations on Powers Granted to the United States]

Limitations on Powers Granted to the Confederacy

[Slave Trade]
Clause 1. The migration or importation of such persons as any of the States now existing shall think proper to admit, shall not be prohibited by the Congress prior to the year one thousand eight hundred and eight, but a tax or duty may be imposed on such importation, not exceeding ten dollars for each person.

No Slave Trade

[Habeas Corpus]
[A law requiring that a detained person be brought before a court at a stated time and place to determine the legality of his detainment]
Clause 2. The privilege of the writ of habeas corpus shall not

No Jails or Prisons
[Since there were no jails or prisons, laws related to detainment were not necessary.]

U. S. CONSTITUTION	GREAT LAW OF PEACE
be suspended, unless when in cases of rebellion or invasion the public safety may require it.	
[Ex Post Facto Law] [A law which has a retroactive effect after the fact] **Clause 3**. No bill of attainder or ex post facto law shall be passed.	**No Reference to Laws which have an effect after the fact**
[Direct Taxes] **Clause 4**. No capitation, or other direct, tax shall be laid, unless in proportion to the census or enumeration herein before directed to be taken.	**No Taxes**
[Duties on Exports] **Clause 5.** No tax or duty shall be laid on articles exported from any State.	**No Duties on Exports**
[No Commercial Discrimination to Be Made Between States] **Clause 6.** No preference shall be given by any regulation of commerce or revenue to the ports of one State over those of another: nor shall vessels bound to, or from, one State, be obliged to enter, clear, or pay duties in another.	**No Commercial Discrimination to be Made Between the Six Nations**
[Money, How Drawn From Treasury] **Clause 7.** No money shall be drawn from the Treasury, but in consequence of appropriations made by law; and a regular statement and account of the receipts and expenditures of all public money shall be published from time to time.	**No Money**

U. S. CONSTITUTION	GREAT LAW OF PEACE
[Titles of Nobility] **Clause 8**. No title of nobility shall be granted by the United States: and no person holding any office of profit or trust under them, shall, without the consent of the Congress, accept of any present, emolument, office, or title, of any kind whatever, from any king, prince, or foreign State. [For other limitations see Amendments I-X.]	**Titles of Nobility** Wampum 45. The women heirs of the Confederate [Chief Statesmanship] titles shall be called Royaneh (Noble) for all time to come. (61-LXI, TLL). **Wampum 46.** The women of the Forty Eight (now fifty) Royaneh families shall be the heirs of the Authorized Names for all time to come. (95-XII, EUC). **Wampum 47.** If the female heirs of the Confederate [Chief Statesmen's] titles become extinct, the title right shall be given by the [Chief Statesmen] of the Confederacy to the sister family whom they shall elect and that family shall hold the name and transmit it to their (female) heirs, but they shall not appoint any of their sons as a candidate for the title until all the eligible men of the former family shall have died or otherwise have become ineligible (25-XXV, TLL). **Wampum 48.** If all the heirs of the [Chief Statesman] title become extinct, and all the families in the clan, then the title shall be given by the [Chief Statesmen] of the Confederacy so the family in a sister clan whom they shall elect. (26-XXVI, TLL). **Wampum 49.** If any of the Royaneh women, heirs of the titleship, shall wilfully withhold a [Chief Statesmanship] or other title and refuse to bestow it, or if such heirs abandon, forsake or despise their heritage then shall such women be deemed buried and their family extinct. The titleship shall then revert to a sister family or clan upon application and complaint. The [Chief Statesmen] of the Confederacy

shall elect the family or clans which shall in future hold the title. (28-XXVIII, TLL).

Section. 10. [Powers Prohibited to the States]

[Powers Prohibited, Absolutely]
Clause 1. No State shall enter into any treaty, alliance, or confederation; grant letters of marque and reprisal; coin money; emit bills of credit; make any thing but gold and silver coin a tender in payment of debts; pass any bill of attainder, ex post facto law, or law impairing the obligation of contracts, or grant any title of nobility.

[Powers Concerning Duties on Imports or Exports]
Clause 2. No State shall, without the consent of the Congress, lay any imposts or duties on imports or exports, except what may be absolutely necessary for executing it's inspection laws: and the net produce of all duties and imposts, laid by any State on imports or exports, shall be for the use of the Treasury of the United States; and all such laws shall be subject to the revision and control of the Congress.

[Powers Permitted With Consent of Congress]
Clause 3. No State shall, without the consent of Congress, lay any duty of tonnage, keep troops, or ships of war in time of peace, enter into any agreement or compact with another State, or with a foreign power, or engage in war, unless actually invaded,

Powers Prohibited to the Nations

Powers Prohibited, Absolutely
Wampunt 92. If a nation, part of a nation, or more than one nation within the Five [Six] Nations should in any way endeavor to destroy the Great Peace by neglect or violating its laws and resolve to dissolve the Confederacy, such a nation or such nations shall be deemed guilty of treason and called enemies of the Confederacy and the Great Peace. (86-III, EUC).

No Reference

Powers Permitted With Consent of Grand Council
Wamputn 97. Before the real people united their nations, each nation had its council fires. Before the Great Peace their councils were held. The five Council Fires shall continue so burn as before and they are not quenched. The [Chief Statesmen[

or in such imminent danger as will not admit of delay.

ARTICLE. II. [EXECUTIVE DEPARTMENT]

Section. 1. [The President]

[Executive Power Vested in the President -- Term of Office]
Clause 1. The executive power shall be vested in a President of the United States of America. He shall hold his office during the term of four years, and, together with the Vice-President, chosen for the same term, be elected, as follows:

[Appointment and Number of Presidential Electors]
Clause 2. Each State shall appoint, in such manner as the legislature thereof may direct, a number of electors, equal to the whole number of Senators and Representatives to which the State may be entitled in the Congress: but no Senator or Representative, or person holding an office of trust or profit under the United States, shall be appointed an elector.

[Mode of Electing President and Vice-President]
Clause 3. The electors shall meet in their respective States, and vote by ballot for two persons, of whom one at least shall not be an inhabitant of the same State with themselves. And they shall

of each nation in future shall settle their nation's affairs at this council fire governed always by the laws and rules of the council of the Confederacy and by the Great Peace. (90-VII, EUC).

THE FIREKEEPERS ONANDAGA

The Adodarho

Executive Power Entrusted with the Adodarho -- Term of Office
Wampum 3. To you Adodarhoh, the Onondaga cousin [Chief Statesmen], I and the other Confederate [Chief Statesmen] have entrusted the caretaking and the watching of the Five [Six] Nations Council Fire. [The term of office is for life, unless he breaks the Great Law and is impeached or has grounds for retirement.] (4-IV, TLL).

Designation and Number of Adodarho Electors
[The present Adodarho told the author that he is a member of the Eel Clan. The Clan Mother, the grandmothers and the mothers of that clan meet to elect a man endowed with the qualities and character required for the position of Adodarho, the Firekeeper of the Confederacy.]

Mode of Electing Adodarho and other Chief Statesmen
Wampum 32. If a Adodarho or other Chief Statesman] should die while the Council of the Five [Six] Nations is in session the Council shall adjourn for ten days. No Confederate Council

make a list of all the persons voted for, and of the number of votes for each; which list they shall sign and certify, and transmit sealed to the seat of the Government of the United States, directed to the President of the Senate. The President of the Senate shall, in the presence of the Senate and House of Representatives, open all the certificates, and the votes shall then be counted. The person having the greatest number of votes shall be the President, if such number be a majority of the whole number of electors appointed; and if there be more than one who have such majority, and have an equal number of votes, then the House of Representatives shall immediately choose by ballot one of them for President; and if no person have a majority, then from the five highest on the list the said House shall in like manner choose the President. But in choosing the President, the votes shall be taken by States, the Representation from each State having one vote; a quorum for this purpose shall consist of a member or members from two-thirds of the States, and a majority of all the States shall be necessary to a choice. In every case, after the choice of the President, the person having the greatest number of votes of the electors shall be the Vice-President. But if there should remain two or more who have equal votes, the Senate shall choose from them by ballot the Vice-President.
[This paragraph has been superseded by the Twelfth Amendment to Constitution. See also Amendment XX.]

shall sit within ten days of the death of a [Adodarho or other Chief Statesman] of the Confederacy.

If the Three Brothers (the Mohawk, the Onondaga and the Seneca) should lose one of their Lords by death, the Younger Brothers (the Oneida, the Cayuga and Tuscarora) shall come to the surviving [Chief Statesmen] of the Three Brothers on the tenth day and console them . . . And the consolation shall be the reading of the contents of the thirteen shell (wampum) strings of Ayonhwhathah [Hiawatha or "He Who Combs"]. At the termination of this rite a successor shall be appointed, to be appointed by the women heirs of the [Chief Statesmanship] title. If the women are not yet ready to place their nominee before the [Chief Statesmen], the Speaker shall say, "Come let us go out." All shall then leave the Council or the place of gathering. The installation shall then wait until such a time as the women are ready. The Speaker shall lead the way from the house by saying, "Let us depart to the edge of the woods and lie in waiting on our bellies." (22-XXII, TLL).

U. S. CONSTITUTION

[Time of Choosing Electors and Casting electoral Vote]
Clause 4. The Congress may determine the time of choosing the electors, and the day on which they shall give their votes; which day shall be the same throughout the United States.

[Qualifications of President]
Clause 5. No person except a natural born citizen, or a citizen of the United States, at the time of the adoption of this Constitution, shall be eligible to the office of President; neither shall any person be eligible to that office who shall not have attained to the age of thirty five years, and been fourteen years a resident within the United States. [See also

GREAT LAW OF PEACE

Time of Installing a Adodarho or Other Chief Statesman
Wampum 30. The [Chief Statesmen] of the Confederacy may confer the [Chief Statesmanship] title upon a candidate whenever the Great Law is recited, if there be a candidate, for the Great Law speaks all the rules. (44-XLIV, TLL).
Wampum 32. (cont.) When the women title holders shall have chosen one of their sons, the Confederate [Chief Statesmen] will assemble in two places, the Younger Brothers [similar to the House of Representatives] in one place and the Three Older Brothers [similar to the Senate] in another. The [Chief Statesmen] who are to console the mourning [Chief Statesmen] shall choose one of their number to sing the Pacification Hymn as they journey to the sorrowing [Chief Statesmen]. The singer shall lead the way and the [Chief Statesmen] and the people shall follow. When they reach the sorrowing [Chief Statesmen], they shall hail the candidate [Adodarho or other Chief Statesmen] and perform the rite of Conferring the [Adodarho or other Chief States manship] Title. (22-XXII, TLL).

Qualifications of Adodarho
Wampum 53. When the Royaneh women, holders of the [Adodarho] title, select one of their sons as a candidate, they shall select one who is trustworthy, of good character, or honest disposition, one who manages his own affairs, supports his own family, if any, and who has proven a faithful man to his Nation. (64-LXIV, TLL).

Article II, Section I, and Fourteenth Amendment]

[Presidential Succession]
Clause 6. In case of the removal of the President from office, or of his death, resignation, or inability to discharge the powers and duties of the said office, the same shall devolve on the Vice-President, and the Congress may by law provide for the case of removal, death, resignation or inability, both of the President and Vice-President, declaring what officer shall then act as President, and such officer shall act accordingly, until the disability be removed, or a President shall be elected.

Adodarho Succession
Wampum 33. When a Confederate [Chief Statesman, much as the Adodarho] dies, the surviving relatives shall immediately dispatch a messenger, a member of another clan, to the [Chief Statesmen] in another locality. When the runner comes within hailing distance of the locality he shall utter a sad wail, thus: "Kwa-ah, Kwa-ah, Kwa-ah!" The sound shall be repeated three times and then again and again at intervals as many times as the distance may require. When the runner arrives at the settlement the people shall assemble and one must ask him the nature of his sad message. He shall then say, "Let us consider." Then he shall tell them of the death of the [Adodarho]. He shall deliver to them a string of shells (wampum) and say, "Here is the testimony, you have heard the message." He may then return home.

It now becomes the duty of the [Chief Statesmen] of the locality to send runners to other localities and each locality shall send other messengers until all [Chief Statesmen] are notified. Runners shall travel day and night. (23-XXIII, TLL). [No one will take Adodarho's place until a new Adodarho is selected by the women of his clan and he has been installed.]

[Salary of President]
Clause 7. The President shall, at stated times, receive for his services, a compensation, which shall neither be increased nor

No Salary for Adodarho
[The position of Adodarho and other Chief Statesmen are unpaid. The people of their own free will support the needs of their leaders]

diminished during the period for which he shall have been elected, and he shall not receive within that period any other emolument from the United States, or any of them.

[Oath of Office of President]
Clause 8. Before he enter on the execution of his office, he shall take the following oath or affirmation:--"I do solemnly swear (or affirm) that I will faithfully execute the office of President of the United States, and will to the best of my ability, preserve, protect and defend the Constitution of the United States."

Installation of Adodarho
Wampum 28. When a candidate [Chief Statesman] is to be installed he shall furnish four strings of shells (or wampum) one span in length bound together at one end. Such will constitute the evidence of his pledge to the Confederate [Chief Statesmen] that he will live according to the constitution of the Great Peace and exercise justice in all affairs.

When the pledge is furnished the Speaker of the Council must hold the shell strings in his hand and address the opposite side of the Council Fire and he shall commence his address saying: "Now behold him. He has now become a Confederate [Chief Statesman]. See how splendid he looks." An address may then follow. At the end of it he shall send the bunch of shell strings to the opposite side and they shall be received as evidence of the pledge, Then shall the opposite side say:

"We now do crown you with the sacred emblem of the deer's antlers, the emblem of the [Chief Statesmanship]. You shall now become a mentor of the people of the Five [Six] Nations. The thickness of your skin shall be seven spans -- which is to say that you shall be proof against anger, offensive actions and criticism. Your heart shall be filled with peace and good will and your mind filled with a yearning for the welfare of the people of the Confederacy. With endless patience you shall carry out your duty and your firmness shall be tempered with tenderness for your people. Neither anger nor fury shall find lodgement in your mind and all your words and actions shall be marked with calm deliberation. In all of your deliberations in the Confederate Council, in your efforts at law making, in all your official acts, self interest shall be cast into oblivion. Cast not over your shoulder behind you the warnings of the nephews and nieces should they chide you for any error or wrong you may do, but return to the way of the Great Law which is just and right. Look and listen for the welfare of the whole people and have always in view not only the present but also the coming generations, even those whose faces are yet beneath the surface of the ground -- the unborn of the future Nations." (51-LI, TLL).

Wampum 64. At the ceremony of the installation of [Chief Statesman] if there is only one expert speaker and singer of the law and the Pacification Hymn to stand at the council fire, then when this speaker and singer has finished addressing one side of the fire he shall go to the opposite side and reply to his own speech and song. He shall thus act for both sides of the fire until the entire ceremony has been completed. Such a speaker and singer shall be termed the "Two Faced," because he speaks and sings for both sides of the fire. (49-XLIX, TLL).

U. S. CONSTITUTION

Section. 2. [Powers of the President]

Commander-in-Chief
Clause 1. The President shall be Commander-in-Chief of the Army and Navy of the United States, and of the militia of the several States, when called into the actual service of the United States; he may require the opinion, in writing, of the principal officer in each of the executive departments, upon any subject relating to the duties of their respective offices, and he shall have power to grant reprieves and pardons for offenses against the United States, except in cases of impeachment.

[Treaties and Appointments]
Clause 2. He shall have power, by and with the advice and consent of the Senate, to make treaties, provided two thirds of the Senators present concur; and he shall nominate, and by and with the advice and consent of the Senate, shall appoint ambassadors, other public ministers and consuls, judges of the Supreme Court, and all other

GREAT LAW OF PEACE

Powers of the Adodarho, Firekeeper of the Six Nations

Not a War Chief
[Adodarho and the Chief Statesmen are responsible for promoting peace, not war, If the territory of the Confederacy is threatened, the authority to defend the people is transferred to the War Chief].
Wampum 36. The title names of the Chief Confederate [Chief Statesmen's] War Chiefs shall be:
Ayonwaehs, War Chief under Chief Takarihoken (Mohawk)
Kahonwahdironh, War Chief under Chief Odatshedeh (Oneida)
Ayendes, War Chief under Chief Adodarhoh (Onondaga)
Wenenhs, War Chief under Chief Dekaenyonh (Cayuga)
Shoneradowaneh, War Chief under Chief Skanyadariyo (Seneca)

The women heirs of each head [Chief Statesman's] title shall be the heirs of the War Chief's title of their respective [Chief Statesman]. (52-LII, TLL).

The War Chiefs shall be selected from the eligible sons of the female families holding the head [Chief Statesmanship] titles. (53-LIII, TLL).

Treaties and Appointments
[Adodarho alone does not have the power to make treaties. Since decisions are made by consensus, a treaty would require near unanimous agreement of the people and their leaders to become law. In contrast with the representative form democracy under the U.S. Constitution, the Six Nations practice participatory democracy which means the

officers of the United States, whose appointments are not herein otherwise provided for, and which shall be established by law: but the Congress may by law vest the appointment of such inferior officers, as they think proper, in the President alone, in the courts of law, or in the heads of departments.

[Filling Vacancies]
Clause 3. The President shall have power to fill up all vacancies that may happen during the recess of the Senate, by granting commissions which shall expire at the end of their next session.

Section. 3. [Duties of the President]

[Message to Congress -- Adjourn and Call Special Session]
He shall from time to time give to the Congress information of the state of the Union, and recommend to their consideration such measures as he shall judge necessary and expedient; he may, on extraordinary occasions, convene both Houses, or either of them, and in case of disagreement between them, with respect to the time of adjournment, he may adjourn them to such time as he shall think proper; he shall receive ambassadors and other public ministers; he shall take care that the laws be faithfully executed, and shall commission all the officers of the United States. [See also Article I, Section 5.]

people have the right to actively participate in their government.

Adodarho and other Chief Statesman also do not have the power to appoint ambassadors, consuls, judges nor other officials -- the power to select leaders rests with the Clan Mothers and the Women's Councils who also serve somewhat like the Supreme Court.]

Filling Vacancies
[The Clan Mothers and the Women's Councils fill the vacancies. Since they have raised the children from birth, they are trusted to know which adults may best serve the people faithfully.]

Duties of the Adodarho, Firekeeper of the Grand Council
Wampum 3. When the [Chief Statesmen] are assembled the Council Fire shall be kindled, but not with chestnut wood [which throws sparks, symbolizing disturbance], and Adodarhoh shall formally open the Council.

Then shall Adodarhoh and his cousins [Chief Statesmen], the Fire Keepers, announce the subject for discussion.

The Smoke of the Confederate Council Fire shall ever ascend and pierce the sky so that other nations who may be allies may see the Council Fire of the Great Peace.

Adodarho and his cousin [Chief Statesmen] are entrusted with the keeping of the Council Fire. (4-IV, TLL).

Wampum 4. You Adodarho, and your thirteen cousin [Chief Statesmen], shall faithfully keep the space about the Council Fire clean and you shall allow neither dust nor dirt to accumulate. I lay a Long Wing before you as a broom. As a weapon against a crawling creature I lay a staff with you so that you may thrust it away from the Council Fire. If you fail to cast it out then call the rest of the United [Chief Statesmen] to your aid. (3-III, TLL).

Wampum 62. When the Confederate Council of the Five [Six] Nations declares for a reading of the belts of shell calling to mind these laws, they shall provide for the reader a specially made mat woven of the fibers of wild hemp. The mat shall not be used again, for such formality is called the honoring of the importance of the law. (36-XXXVI, TLL).

Wampum 63. Should two sons of opposite sides of the council fire agree in a desire to hear the reciting of the laws of the Great Peace and so refresh their memories in the way ordained by the founder of the Confederacy, they shall notify Adodarho. He then shall consult with five of his coactive [Chief Statesmen] and they in turn shall consult their eight brethren. Then should they decide to accede to the request of the two sons from opposite sides of the Council Fire, Adodarhoh shall send messengers to notify the [Chief Statesmen] of each of the Five [Six] Nations. Then they shall dispatch their War Chiefs to notify their brother and cousin [Chief Statesmen] of the meeting and its time and place.

When all have come and have assembled, Adodarhoh, in conjunction with his cousin [Chief

Statesmen] shall appoint one [Chief Statesman] who shall repeat the laws of the Great Peace. Then shall they announce who they have chosen to repeat the laws of the Great Peace to the two sons. Then shall the chosen one repeat the laws of the Great Peace. (43-XLIII, TLL).

Section. 4. [Removal of Executive and Civil Officers]

[Impeachment of President and Other Officers]
The President, Vice-President and all civil officers of the United States, shall be removed from office on impeachment for, and conviction of, treason, bribery, or other high crimes and misdemeanors. [See also Article I, Sections 2 and 3]

Removal of Chiefs and Other Officials

Impeachment of a Chief
[If a Chief acts against the People or in a way unbecoming the dignity of his position, a Clan Mother shall send a messenger to warn him. However, if the Chief does not correct himself immediately, a Clan Mother has the power to impeach him at once. If a Chief fails to yield to the will of the Clan Mother, she may order enforcement from a special prosecutor known as the "One Who Gives No Mercy.]

ARTICLE III. [JUDICIAL DEPARTMENT]

Section. 1. [Judicial Powers Vested in federal Courts]

[Courts -- Terms of Office and Salary of Judges]
The judicial power of the United States, shall be vested in one Supreme Court, and in such Inferior Courts as the Congress may from time to time ordain and establish. The judges, both of the Supreme and Inferior Courts, shall hold their offices during good behaviour, and shall, at stated times, receive for

JUDICIAL COUNCILS

Judicial Powers Vested in the Women's Councils, Men's Council's and the General Council Fires of the People

Council Fires -- Terms of Service and Compensation of Clan Mothers
[The judicial power of the Confederacy is endowed largely in the Women's Councils led by the Clan Mothers who serve for life, subject to good behavior. They receive no money for their service.] **Wampum 95.** The women of every clan of the Five [Six] Nations shall have a Council Fire ever

their services, a compensation, which shall not be diminished during their continuance in office.

Section. 2. [Jurisdiction of United States Courts]

[Cases That May Come Before United States Courts]

Clause 1. The judicial power shall extend to all cases, in law and equity, arising under this Constitution, the laws of the United States, and treaties made, or which shall be made, under their authority; --to all cases affecting ambassadors, other public ministers and consuls; --to all cases of admiralty and maritime jurisdiction; --to controversies to which the United States shall be a party; --to controversies between two or more States; --between a State and citizens of another State; --between citizens of different States, --between citizens of the same State claiming lands under grants of different States, and between a State, or the

burning in readiness for a council of the clan. When in their opinion it seems necessary for the interest of the people they shall hold a council and their decision and recommendation shall be introduced before the Council of [Chief Statesmen] by the War Chief for its consideration. (87-IV, EUC).

Wampum 94. The men of every clan of the Five [Six] Nations shall have a Council Fire ever burning in readiness for a council of the clan. When it seems necessary for a council to be held to discuss the welfare of the clans, then the men may gather about the fire. This council shall have the same rights as the council of the women (88-V, EUC).

Jurisdiction of Confederacy Council Fires

Matters That May Come Before Confederacy Council Fires

Wampum 93. Whenever a specially important matter or a great emergency is presented before the Confederate Council and the nature of the matter affects the entire body of Five [Six] Nations, threatening their utter ruin, then the [Chief Statesmen] of the Confederacy must submit the matter to the decision of the people and the decision of the people shall affect the decision of the Confederate Council. This decision shall be a confirmation of the voice of the people. (84-XV, SPW).

citizens thereof, and foreign States, citizens or subjects. [See also Eleventh Amendment]

[Jurisdiction of Supreme and Appellate Courts]
Clause 2. In all cases affecting ambassadors, other public ministers and consuls, and those in which a State shall be party, the Supreme Court shall have original jurisdiction. In all the other cases before mentioned, the Supreme Court shall have appellate jurisdiction, both as to law and fact, with such exceptions, and under such regulations as the Congress shall make.

Jurisdiction of the General Council and Clan Council Fires
Wampum 96. All the Clan council fires of a nation or the Five [Six] Nations may unite into one general council fire, or delegates from all the council fires may be appointed to unite in a general council for discussing the interests of the people. The people shall have the right to make appointments and to delegate their power to others of their number. When their council shall have come to a conclusion on any matter, their decision shall be reported to the Council of the Nation or to the Confederate Council (as the case may require) by the War Chief or the War Chiefs. (89-VI, EUC).

[Trial of Crimes]
Clause 3. The Trial of all crimes, except in cases of impeachment, shall be by jury; and such trial shall be held in the State where the said crimes shall have been committed; but when not committed within any State, the trial shall be at such place or places as the Congress may by law have directed. [See also Fifth, Sixth, Seventh, and Eighth Amendments.]

Counselling Those Who Break the Great Law
[If a person breaks the law, the matter may first be addressed by the person's mother and father, then grandmothers and grandfathers who offer counselling. A more serious or repeat offender may require a counselling from the Clan Mother and Women's Council and/or Men's Council. An even more serious matter could go to the Nation's Council and/or Confederacy Council. However, if the person is suffering from a mental or spiritual disorder, certain Medicine Societies may be needed to heal the person. Since no prisons exist, a person who was impossible to reform might be banished from the territory.]

U. S. CONSTITUTION	GREAT LAW OF PEACE
Section. 3. [Treason]	**Treason**
[Treason Defined] **Clause 1.** Treason against the United States, shall consist only in levying war against them, or in adhering to their enemies, giving them aid and comfort.	**Treason Defined** **Wampum 92.** If a nation, part of a nation, or more than one nation within the Five [Six] Nations should in any way endeavor to destroy the Great Peace by neglect or violating its laws and resolve to dissolve the Confederacy, such a nation or such nations shall be deemed guilty of treason and called enemies of the Confederacy and the Great Peace.
[Conviction] **Clause 1. (cont.)** No person shall be convicted of treason unless on the testimony of two witnesses to the same overt act, or on confession in open court.	**Conviction** **Wampum 92. (cont.)** It shall then be the duty of [Chief Statesmen] who remain faithful to resolve to warn the offending people.
[Punishment] **Clause 2.** The Congress shall have power to declare the punishment of treason, but no attainder of treason shall work corruption of blood, or forfeiture except during the life of the person attained.	**Punishment** **Wampum 92. (cont.)** They shall be warned once and if a second warning is necessary they shall be driven from the territory of the Confederacy by the War Chiefs and his men. (86-III, EUC).
ARTICLE. IV. [THE STATES AND THE FEDERAL GOVERNMENT]	**THE CLANS, NATIONS AND THE CONFEDERATE GRAND COUNCIL**
Section. 1. [Official Acts of the States]	**Sanctioned Acts of the Nations, Clans and People**
Full Faith and Credit Full Faith and Credit shall be given in each State to the public acts, records, and judicial proceedings of every other State. And the Congress may by general laws prescribe the manner in which such acts, records and proceedings shall be proved, and the	**Being of One head, One Body and One Mind** A large bunch of shell strings [50], in the making of which the Five [Six] Nations Confederate [Chief Statesmen] have equally contributed, shall symbolize the completeness of the union and certify the pledge of the nations represented by the

effect thereof. [See also fourteenth Amendment.]

[The U.S. adopted this symbolism in the National Seal which features an eagle holding thirteen arrows representing the original 13 states.]

Confederate [Chief Statesmen] of the Mohawk, the Oneida, the Onondaga, the Cayuga and the Seneca [and the Tuscarora], that are all united and formed into one body or union called the Union of the Great Law, which they have established . . . (14-XIV, TLL).

Wampum 56. Five strings of shell tied together as one shall represent the Five Nations. Each string shall represent one territory and the whole a completed united territory known as the Five Nations Confederate territory. (l08-XXV, EUC).

Wampum 57. Five arrows shall be bound together very strong and each arrow shall represent one nation. Thus are the Five Nations united completely and enfolded together, united into one head, one body and one mind. Therefore they shall labor, legislate and council together for the interest of future generation . . . (I5-XV, TLL).

Section. 2. [Citizens of the States]

[Interstate Privileges of Citizens]

Clause 1. The citizens of each State shall be entitled to all privileges and immunities of citizens in the several States.

Citizens of the Nations International Privileges of Citizens

Wampum 59. A bunch of wampum shells on strings, three spans of the hand in length, the upper half of the bunch being white and the lower half black, and formed from equal contributions of the men [and women] of the Five [Six] Nations, shall be a token that the men [and women] have combined themselves into one head, one body and one thought, and it shall also symbolize their ratification of the peace pact of the Confederacy, whereby the [Chief Statesmen] of the Five

[Six] have established the Great Peace.

The white portion of the shell strings represent the women and the black portion the men . . . (81-SPW, XII).

[Fugitives From Justice]
Clause 2. A person charged in any State with treason, felony, or other crime, who shall flee from justice, and be found in another State, shall on demand of the executive authority of the State from which he fled, be delivered up, to be removed to the State having jurisdiction of the crime.

Fugitives From Justice
No Reference

[Fugitives From Service]
Clause 3. No person held to service or labour in one State, under the laws thereof, escaping into another, shall, in consequence of any law or regulation therein, be discharged from such service or labour, but shall be delivered up on claim of the party to whom such service or labour may be due. ["Person" here includes slave. This was the basis of the fugitive Slave laws of 1793 and 1850. It is now superseded by the Thirteenth Amendment, by which slavery is prohibited.]

Fugitives From Service
No Reference

Section. 3. [New States]

[Admission or Division of States]
Clause 1. New States may be admitted by the Congress into this Union; but no new State shall be formed or erected within the jurisdiction of any other State; nor any State be formed by the junction of two or more States, or parts of States, without the consent of the legislatures of the

New Nations, Clans and Citizens Adoption of Nations, Clans and People
Wampum 66. The father of a child of great comliness, learning, ability or specially loved because of some circumstance may, at the will of the child's clan, select a name from his own (the father's) clan and bestow it by ceremony, such as is provided. This naming shall be only temporary and

States concerned as well as of the Congress.

shall be called, "A name hung about the neck." (96-XII, EUC)

Wampum 67. Should any person, a member of the Five [Six] Nation's Confederacy, specially esteem a man or a woman of another clan or of a foreign nation, he may choose a name and bestow it upon that person so esteemed. The naming shall be in accord with the ceremony of bestowing names . . . A short string of shell shall be delivered with the name as a record and a pledge. (97-XIV, EUC).

Wampum 68. Should any member of the Five [Six] Nations, family or person belonging to a foreign nation submit a proposal for adoption into a clan of one of the Five [Six] Nations, he or they shall furnish a string of shells, span in length, as a pledge to the clan into which he or they wish to be adopted. The [Chief Statesmen] of the nation shall then consider the proposal and submit a decisions. (104-XXI, EUC).

Wampum 69. Any member of the Five [Six] Nations who through esteem or other feeling wishes to adopt an individual, a family, or number of families may offer adoption to him or them and if accepted the matter shall be brought to the attention of the [Chief Statesmen] must confirm the adoption. (105-XXII, EUC).

Wampum 70. When the adoption of anyone shall have been confirmed by the [Chief Statesmen] of the Nation, the [Chief Statesmen] shall address the people of their nation and say: "Now you of our nation, be informed that such a person, such a family or such families have ceased forever to hear their birth nation's name and have buried it in the depths of the earth. Henceforth let no one of our nation ever mention the original name or nation of their birth. To do so will be to hasten the end of our peace." (106-XXIII, EUC).

Wampum 77. When the [Chief Statesmen] of the Confederacy decide to admit a foreign nation and an adoption is made, the [Chief Statesmen] shall inform the adopted nation that its admission is only temporary. They shall also say to the nation that it must never try to control, to interfere with or to injure the Five [Six] Nations nor disregard the Great Peace or any of its rules or customs. That in no way should they cause disturbance or injury. Then should the adopted nation disregard these injunctions, their adoption shall be annulled and they shall be expelled . . . (122-XXXIX, EUC).

[Control of the Property and Territory of the Union]

Clause 2. The Congress shall have power to dispose of and make all needful rules and regulations respecting the territory or other property belonging to the United States; and nothing in this Constitution shall be so construed as to prejudice any claims of the United States, or of any particular State.

Birthright to the Property and Territory of the People

Wampum 73. The soil of the earth from one end of the land to the other is the property of the people who inhabit it. By birthright the Ongwehonweh (Original beings) are the owners of the soil which they own and occupy and none other may hold it. The same law has been held from the oldest times.

The Great Creator has made us of the one blood and of the same soil he made us and as only different tongues constitute different nations he established different hunting grounds and territories and made boundary lines between them. (69-LXIX; TLL).

Section. 4. [Protection of States Guaranteed]

[Republican Form of Government]
The United States shall guarantee to every State in this Union a republican form of government, and shall protect each of them against invasion; and on application of the legislature, or of the executive (when the legislature cannot be convened) against domestic violence.

Protection of the People Guaranteed

Participatory Democratic Form of Government
Wampum 58. There are now the Five [Six) Nations Confederate Chief Statesmen] standing with joined hands in a circle . . . You, the Five [Six] Nations be firm so that if a tree falls upon your joined arms it shall not separate you or weaken your hold. So shall the strength of the union be preserved. (16-XIV, TLL).

ARTICLE. V. [AMENDMENTS]

[Amendments, How Proposed and Adopted]
The Congress, whenever two-thirds of both Houses shall deem it necessary, shall propose Amendments to this Constitution, or, on the application of the legislatures of two-thirds of the several States, shall call a convention for proposing amendments, which, in either case, shall be valid to all intents and purposes, as part of this Constitution, when ratified by the Legislatures of three-fourths of the several States, or by conventions in three-fourths thereof, as the one or the other mode of ratification may be proposed by the Congress; provided that no amendment which may be made prior to the year one thousand eight hundred and eight shall in any manner affect the first and fourth clauses in the ninth section

ADDING TO THE RAFTERS

Adding to the Rafters, How Proposed and Adopted
Wampum 16. If the conditions which shall arise at any future time call for an addition to or change of this law, the case shall be carefully considered and if a new beam seems necessary or beneficial, the proposed changed shall be voted upon and if adopted it shall be called, "Added to the Rafters." (48-XLVII, TLL.)

U. S. CONSTITUTION	GREAT LAW OF PEACE
of the first article; and that no State, without its consent, shall be deprived of its equal suffrage in the Senate.	
ARTICLE. VI. [GENERAL PROVISIONS]	**GENERAL PROVISIONS**
[The Public Debt] **Clause 1.** All debts contracted and engagements entered into, before the adoption of this Constitution, shall be as valid against the United States under this Constitution, as under the Confederation. [See also Fourteenth Amendment, Section 4.]	**No Public Debt**
[Supreme Law of the Land] **Clause 2.** This Constitution, and the laws of the United States which shall be made in pursuance thereof; and all treaties made, or which shall be made, under the authority of the United States, shall be the supreme law of the land; and the judges in every State shall be bound thereby, any thing in the Constitution or laws of any State to the contrary notwithstanding.	**Supreme Law of the Land** **Wampum 60.** A broad dark belt of wampum of thirty-eight rows, having a white heart in the center, on either side of which are two white squares all connected with the heart by white rows of beads shall be emblem of the unity of the Five [Six] Nations. [Known as the "Hiawatha Belt."] The first of the square on the left represents the Mohawk nation and its territory; the second square on the left and the one near the heart, represents the Oneida nation and its territory; the white heart in the middle represent the Onondaga nation and its territory, and it also means the heart of the Five Nations is single in its loyalty to the Great Peace, that the Great Peace is lodged in the heart (meaning with Onondaga Confederate [Chief Statesmen]), and that the Council Fire is to burn there for the Five Nations, and further, it means that the authority is given to advance the cause of peace

whereby hostile nations out of the Confederacy shall cease warfare; the white square to the right of the heart represents the Cayuga nation and its territory and the fourth and last white square represents the Seneca nation and its territory.

White shall here symbolize that no evil or jealous thoughts shall creep into the minds of the [Chief Statesmen] while in council under the Great Peace. White, the emblem of peace, love, charity and equity surrounds and guards the Five [Six] Nations. (84-I, EUC).

[Oaths of Office -- No Religious Test Required]

Clause 3. The Senators and Representatives before mentioned, and the members of the several State Legislatures, and all executive and judicial officers, both of the United States and of the several States, shall be bound by oath or affirmation, to support this Constitution; but no religious test shall ever be required as a qualification to any office or public trust under the United States.

Chief Statesmen Are Both Civil and Religious Leaders

Wampum 100. It shall be the duty of the [Chief Statesmen] of each brotherhood to confer at the approach of the time of the Mid-winter Thanksgiving and to notify their people of the approaching festival. They shall hold a council over the matter and arrange its details and begin the Thanksgiving five days after the moon of Dis-ko-nah is new. The people shall assemble at the appointed place and the nephews shall notify the people of the time and the place from the beginning to the end the [Chief Statesmen] shall preside over the Thanksgiving and address the people from time to time. (100-XVII, EUC).

Wampum 101. It shall be the duty of the appointed managers of the Thanksgiving festivals to do all that is needful for carrying out the duties of the occasions.

The recognized festivals of Thanksgiving shall be the Thanksglving, the Maple or Sugar-making Thanksgiving, the

Raspberry Thanksgiving, the Strawberry Thanksgiving, the Corn-planting Thanksgiving, the Corn Hoeing Thanksgiving, the Little Festival of Green Corn, the Great Festival of Ripe Corn and the complete Thanksgiving for the Harvest.

Each nation's festivals shall be held in their Long Houses. (101-XVIII, EUC).

ARTICLE. VII. [RATIFICATION OF THE CONSTITUTION]

[Ratification of Nine States Required]
The Ratification of the conventions of nine States, shall be sufficient for the establishment of this Constitution between the States so ratifying the same.

DONE in Convention by the unanimous consent of the States present the seventeenth day of September in the year of our Lord one thousand seven hundred and eighty seven and of the Independence of the United States of America the twelfth in witness whereof we have hereunto subscribed our names.
George Washington-- Presidt and deputy from Virginia (et.al.)

PLEDGE TO UPHOLD THE GREAT LAW OF PEACE

Burying All Weapons of War Beneath the Tree of Peace
Wampum 65. I, [the Peacemaker], and the Union [Chief Statesmen], now uproot the tallest pine tree and into the cavity thereby made, we cast all weapons of war. Into the depths of the earth, down into the deep underearth currents of water flowing to unknown regions we cast all the weapons of strife. We bury them from sight and we plant again the tree. Thus shall the Great Peace be established and hostilities shall no longer be known between the Five [Six] Nations but peace to the United People.

AMENDMENTS

AMENDMENT I [Restrictions on Powers of Congress]
Congress shall make no law respecting an establishment of religion, or prohibiting the free exercise thereof; or abridging the freedom of speech, or of the press; or the right of the people peaceably to assemble, and to petition the

ADDING TO THE RAFTERS

Wampum 99. Religious Ceremonies Protected
The rites and festival of each nation shall remain undisturbed and shall continue as before because they were given by the people of old times as useful and necessary for the good of men [and women]. (99-XVL, TLL).

U. S. CONSTITUTION	GREAT LAW OF PEACE
Government for a redress of grievances.	**Wampum 102.** When the Thanksgiving for the Green Corn come the special managers, both men and women, shall give it careful attention and do their duties property. (102-XIX, EUC). **Wumpum 103.** When the Ripe Corn Thanksgiving is celebrated the [Chief Statesmen] of the Nation must give it the same attention as they give to the Midwinter Thanksgiving. (103-XX, EUC). **Wampum 104.** Whenever any man [or woman] proves himself [or herself] by his [or her] good life and his [or her] knowledge of good things, naturally fitted as a teacher of good things, he [or she] shall be recognized by the [Chief Statesmen] as a teacher of peace and religion and the people shall hear him or [her]. (93-X, EUC).
AMENDMENT II **[Right to Bear Arms]** A well regulated militia, being necessary to the security of a free State, the right of the people to keep and bear arms, shall not be infringed.	**Weapons of War** **Buried Beneath the Tree of Peace**
AMENDMENT III **[Billeting of Soldiers]** No soldier shall, in time of peace be quartered in any house, without the consent of the owner, nor in time of war, but in a manner to be prescribed by law.	**Protection of the House** **Wampum 107.** A certain sign shall be known to all the people of the Five [Six] Nations which shall denote that the owner or occupant of a house is absent. A stick or pole in a slanting or leaning position shall indicate this and be the sign. Every person not entitled to enter the house by right of living within it upon seeing such a sign shall not approach the house either by day or by night but shall keep as far away

as his business will permit. (92-IX, EUC).

AMENDMENT IV
[Seizures, Searches and Warrants]
The right of the people to be secure in their persons, houses, papers, and effects, against unreasonable searches and seizures, shall not be violated, and no warrants shall issue, but upon probable cause, supported by oath or affirmation, and particularly describing the place to be searched, and the persons or things to be seized.

No Reference

AMENDMENT V
[Criminal Proceedings and Condemnation of Property]
No person shall be held to answer for a capital, or otherwise infamous crime, unless on a presentment or indictment of a Grand Jury, except in cases arising in the land or naval forces, or in the militia, when in actual service in time of war or public danger; nor shall any person be subject for the same offence to be twice put in jeopardy of life or limb; nor shall be compelled in any criminal case to be a witness against himself, nor be deprived of life, liberty, or property, without due process of law; nor shall private property be taken for public use, without just compensation.

No Reference

AMENDMENT VI
[Mode of Trial in Criminal Proceedings]
In all criminal prosecutions, the accused shall enjoy the right to a speedy and public trial, by an impartial jury of the State and district wherein the crime shall

No Reference

have been committed, which district shall have been previously ascertained by law, and to be informed of the nature and cause of the accusation; to be confronted with the witnesses against him; to have compulsory process for obtaining witnesses in his favor, and to have the assistance of counsel for his defense.

AMENDMENT VII
[Trial by Jury]
In Suits at common law, where the value in controversy shall exceed twenty dollars, the right of trial by jury shall be preserved, and no fact tried by a jury, shall be otherwise re-examined in any court of the United States, than according to the rules of the common law.

Hearing Before Council Fire
Wampums 93-98. [The people have the right to be heard before the Council Fires of the men of their clan, the women of their clan, the Chief Statesmen of their nation, as well as the Chief Statesmen of the Confederacy.]

AMENDMENT VIII
[Bails -- Fines -- Punishments]
Excessive bail shall not be required, nor excessive fines imposed, nor cruel and unusual punishments inflicted.

No Bails -- Wampum Compensation -- Punishments
[The concept of bail is foreign. Wampum Compensation is for repayment of crimes to overcome the desire for revenge, especially to prevent blood revenge involving capital crimes.]

AMENDMENT IX
[Certain Rights Not Denied to the People]
The enumeration in the Constitution, of certain rights, shall not be construed to deny or disparage others retained by the people.

WAMPUM
Certain Rights Not Denied to the People
This string of wampum vest the people with the right to correct their erring [Chief Statesmen] in case a part of all the [Chief Statesmen] pursue a course not vouched for by the people and heed not the third warning of their women relatives, then the matter shall be taken to the General Council of the women of the Five [Six] Nations. If the [Chief Statesmen] notified and

warned three times fail to heed, then the case falls into the hands of the men of the Five [Six] Nations. The War Chiefs shall then, by right of such power and authority, enter the open council to warn the [Chief Statesmen] to return from their wrong course. If the Lords heed the warning they shalt say, "we will reply tomorrow." If then an answer is returned in favor of justice and in accord with this Great Law, then the [Chief Statesmen] shall individually pledge themselves again by again furnishing the necessary shells for the pledge. Then shall the War Chief or Chiefs exhort the [Chief Statesmen] urging them to be just and true . . . (81-SPW, XII).

Wampum 61. Should a great calamity threaten the generations rising and living of the Five [Six] United Nations, then he who is able to climb to the top of the Tree of the Great Long Leaves may do so. When then, he reaches the top of the Tree he shall look about in all directions and, should he see that evil things indeed are approaching, then he shall call to the people of the Five [Six] United Nations assembled beneath the Tree of the Great Long Leaves and say:

"A calamity threatens your happiness.

Then shall the [Chief Statesmen] convene in council and discuss the impending evil.

When all the truths relating to the trouble shall be fully known and found to be truths, then shall the people seek out a Tree of Ka-hon-ka-ah-go-nah [Great Swamp Elm), and when they shall find it they shall assemble their heads together and lodge for a time between its roots. Then their labors being finished, they may hope for happiness for many days after. (85-II, EUC).

AMENDMENT X
[State Rights]
The powers not delegated to the United States by the Constitution, nor prohibited by it to the States, are reserved to the States respectively, or to the people.

HUMAN, FAMILY, CLAN, NATIONAL AND NATURAL RIGHTS
[Ever human being who is a member of a family, clan and a nation has certain responsibilities and rights. Everyone has a responsibility to help protect and to preserve the earth, Our Mother, for the benefit of her children seven generations to come. Everyone has the right to be free to come and to go, free to live in harmony with the laws of nature, free to enjoy liberty to exist in a natural way, as long as one continues to gives thanks for all land and life.]

Testimony

Testimony of Dr. Gregory Schaaf in behalf of the Iroquois Confederacy before the United States Senate Select Committee for Indian Affairs (December 7, 1986).

I would like to thank you very much for inviting us here today. I am a young historian, and I have dedicated myself to studying the roots of democracy and the history of this land.

I must say that I was very impressed at the end of the Iran-Contra hearings when you gave your concluding remarks, Senator [Daniel Inouye], when you said that much as the Constitutional Convention was presented with different views of the relationship of government and its citizens of 200 years ago, it is our form of government which is what gives us our strength. I think you were absolutely right. It is our form of government that gives us our strength.

As an historian, I have been searching back for the roots of that form of government. What are the origins of democracy within this land? What are the roots of democracy on Earth?

As I have traced through the historical records, I have found that those roots trace back to where this gentleman on my right, Chief Oren Lyons, comes from the Haudenosaunee, the Iroquois Confederacy.

I began researching the history of the confederacy and the relationship to the United States government 11 years ago when I uncovered a collection of original unpublished documents called the Morgan Papers. They included previously unknown letters written by George Washington, Thomas Jefferson, John Hancock, papers related to Benjamin Franklin, Patrick Henry, and also the private journal of George Morgan who was one of the first Indian agents for the Continental Congress and helped to negotiate the first U.S.-Indian peace treaty in 1776.

I used to keep a time log of my research into this topic that is before this committee today. A few years ago, I got up to 10,000 hours and I just quit counting. The evidence is overwhelming. I swear to you, my leader, I swear to the American people, I swear to the people from all around the world that the evidence to support S. Con. Res. 76 is overwhelming. I have presented about 75 pages of written testimony, but we could have presented thousands and thousands of pages.

On April 19, 1776, John Hancock and Congress appointed George Morgan to be their Indian agent. They told him at that time that he was required to provide that a great peace belt, a peace belt with 13 diamonds and 2,500 wampum beads be delivered to the leaders of the western Indian nations. Our ancestors took that peace belt and delivered it to Chief Oren Lyons' ancestors. There was a duplicate belt that was also delivered to the Lenni Lenape or Delaware Nation who are the grandfathers of the Algonquin family of nations.

At that time, the Iroquois and Algonquin peoples and the other Indian nations of this land truly held a balance of power within their hands. If they at that crucial juncture in time as the birth of America was about to emerge had joined the British and attacked from the west as the British attacked from the east, the revolution clearly could have been crushed, and these United States of America might not have been created as we enjoy our rights and liberties under the Constitution today.

Just before the founding fathers were about to make their Declaration of Independence, a delegation of his ancestors came before Congress. They came there to recognize the United States that was about to be born. They also were opening diplomatic relations between the revolutionary government and their own government.

John Hancock and the Members of Congress were so impressed by the ideas of democracy as expressed by these chiefs that I would like to share with you what John Hancock said on that day in 1776. He began by addressing his ancestors as brothers, because the original relationship between the United States Government and the Indian nations was a brother-to-brother relationship, a shoulder-to-shoulder relationship.

And John Hancock said to the Iroquois ambassadors, "We hope the friendship that is between us and you will be firm and continue as long as the sun shall shine and the waters run, that we and you may be as one people and have but one heart and be kind to one another like brethren."

When George Morgan, being the Indian agent representing the United States, addressed the Indian nations, he said to them:

> Brothers, we are not only inclined to do you justice in all things, but we wish to promote your happiness

> and to render you every service in our power if you tell us what you want. We therefore desire you to be wise and that your wise people will consider this matter well, for we wish to see you a happy people and to live with you in friendship forever. Speak your minds free when you come to the treaty that we may understand you.

I think that the freedom of speech is something that is fundamental to our society. It is one of the things that makes us great as a people.

The Onondaga ambassadors conveyed to John Hancock an Indian name. They called him Karandawan which, roughly translated, means "The Great Tree of Liberty." The Tree of Peace which Chief Lyons so eloquently described under which the Great Peacemaker inspired the warriors to bury their weapons which may be the oldest historical evidence of an effort for disarmament in the history of the world and then placed atop of it this sacred Tree of Peace that Tree of Peace became a symbol for the American revolutionaries and became the Tree of Liberty.

Atop that tree is the eagle, and as we look at the flag of these United States of America that is to your right, Senator, on top of it we see that eagle. Before you there is a wooden carving, and it shows the eagle which is part of our national symbol. Within his talons is an olive branch that symbolizes the tree as a symbol of peace.

Also in his talons are these arrows, and part of what the Peacemaker did was he said that each nation represented like an arrow, and one arrow standing alone might be broken easily, but he bound the five nations together, symbolized by the five arrows.

That was something that was impressed upon our founding fathers. So, when they were designing our national emblem, they took this model from the Haudenosaunee. That is why in this wooden emblem that is before you we see these arrows that are bound in the eagle's talons.

At the very first Indian-US peace treaty in 1776, there were certain promises that were made to the Indian nations. Our government promised their governments that we would always respect their land rights. We promised that we would respect their right to justice. We also promised that their young men would never have to fight in our wars unless they volunteered to do so. Many of them have done so. There were Indian people who fought in the Revolutionary War, in the War of 1812, in the Civil War, as well as World War I and World

War II, Korea, and Viet Nam. They have fought to defend this land.

Also, they should, I believe, have retained that right to serve as they wish. I think also of the treaties themselves, what is the Constitution? To me, the Constitution of the United States is like a treaty between we the people and our government. I think that the Senate resolution is so important to be passed because I think it will give a message to the world that we of the United States Government really honor our treaties, our treaties with the Indian nations, our treaties with our allies, and also the treaty that we are about to sign with the Soviet Union.

I think that S. Con. Res. 76 is kind of a model of understanding. I think, too, as I have looked into the U.S. Constitution and compared it with the Iroquois Great Law of Peace, one of the things that we did was we took the U.S. Constitution and we placed it in one column. Then, side-by-side, we selected appropriate clauses from the Iroquois Great Law of Peace.

I was absolutely astounded, Senator, by the similarities between the documents, the separation of powers, the divisions of our government. The fundamental structure of the United States Government clearly was modeled on the Iroquois Grand Council.

Also, I think some of the differences were very interesting -- fundamentally, the rights of women. I think that if the entire Great Law of Peace had been adopted in greater entirety within the U.S. Constitution, women within this land would not have had to wait so long to have had the right to vote. They would not have had to wait so long to have fundamental rights.

I think also that the qualifications of leadership are very important. One of the qualities of leadership within the Iroquois society is that, first and foremost, their leaders must be honest in all things.

I think that in your remarks at the recent Iran-Contra hearings, I must tell you that it really helped to reinforce my sense of patriotism, my sense of pride in America. You underscored the fundamental principles of this land.

Having researched very carefully and continuing to research--because I am a very young man--the fundamental principles of democracy, I think that it is the right of we the people to have the freedom of speech, the freedom of expression, that if we as a people express those rights and really live up to those principles, it will create a model for people all around the world.

I think also within the Constitution the commerce clause is very important, and its relationship with taxation or the exclusion of taxation towards Native people.

In conclusion, I would like to say that the Iroquois, the Haudenosaunee Grand Council is perhaps the oldest participatory democracy on earth. I spent three hours presenting the evidence before the National Indian Education Association. This is a body of over 1000 of the top Indian educators in the country.

They unanimously passed a resolution supporting S. Con. Res. 76. They also felt it was very important that the curriculum for our public school systems from kindergarten through grade 12 to the university level must now be rewritten. This history of this land must be rewritten to recognize the remarkable contributions of the original people of this land.

To symbolize that, Native peoples are planting trees as symbols of peace all across this land. They have planted trees of peace at the State Capitol in California, at the State Capitol in New York. Next September, there will be a tree of peace planted on the Mall here in Washington that I hope you may be able to attend. Perhaps there might be a tree of peace planted in your home State, in Washington, and in every State of this Union and every capitol on this earth, because my grandpa told me to dream for the best but always be prepared for the least.

At the very best, perhaps the dream of the Peacemaker, a world without war might one day come true, but at the very least, we will plant many beautiful trees upon this earth and spread the fundamental principles of democracy in this land.

Thank you very much.

The CHAIRMAN [Senator Daniel Inouye responded]. "I thank you very much, Dr. Schaaf, for your eloquence."

100TH CONGRESS
1ST SESSION

S. CON. RES. 76

To acknowledge the contribution of the Iroquois Confederacy of Nations to the development of the United States Constitution and to reaffirm the continuing government-to-government relationship between Indian tribes and the United States established in the Constitution.

IN THE SENATE OF THE UNITED STATES

SEPTEMBER 16, 1987

Mr. INOUYE (for himself, Mr. Evans, Mr. DECONCINI, Mr. BURDICK, Mr. MCCAIN, Mr. ADAMS, Mr. BOREN, Mr. CONRAD, Mr. CRANSTON, Mr. D'AMATO, Mr. DOLE, Mr. FORD, Mr. FOWLER, Mr. LEVIN, Mr. PELL, Mr. PRYOR, Mr. REID, Mr. RIEGLE, and Mr. STAFFORD) submitted the following concurrent resolution; which was referred to the Select Committee on Indian Affairs

---

CONCURRENT RESOLUTION

To acknowledge the contribution of the Iroquois Confederacy of Nations to the development of the United States Constitution and to reaffirm the continuing government-to-government relation ship between Indian tribes and the United States established in the Constitution.

Whereas the original framers of the Constitutions, including most notably, George Washington and Benjamin Franklin, are known to have greatly admired the concepts, principles and governmental practices of the Six Nations of the Iroquois Confederacy; and,

Whereas the confederation of the original Thirteen Colonies into one republic was explicitly modeled upon the Iroquois Confederacy as were many of the democratic principles which were incorporated into the Constitution itself; and,

Whereas since the formation of the United States, the Congress has recognized the sovereign status of Indian tribes, and has, through the exercise of powers reserved to the Federal Government in the Commerce Clause of the Constitution (art. I, s8, cl.3), dealt with Indian tribes on a government-to-government basis and has, through the treaty clause (art. II, s2, cl.2) entered into three hundred and seventy treaties with Indian tribal nations; and,

Whereas from the first treaty entered into with an Indian nation, the treaty with the Delaware Indians of September 17, 1778, and thereafter in every Indian treaty until the cessation of treaty making in 1871, the Congress has assumed a trust responsibility and obligation to Indian tribes and their members to "exercise the utmost good faith in dealings with the Indians" as provided for in the Northwest Ordinance of 1787, (1 Stat. 50); and,

Whereas Congress has consistently reaffirmed these fundamental policies over the past two hundred years through legislation specifically designed to honor this special relationship; and,

Whereas the judicial system of the United States has consistently recognized and reaffirmed this special relationship; Now, therefore, be it *Resolved by the Senate (the House of Representatives concurring)*, That--

(1) the Congress, on the occasion of the two hundredth anniversary of the signing of the Unites States Constitution, acknowledges the historical debt which his Republic of the United States of America owes to the Iroquois Confederacy and other Indian nations for their demonstration of enlightened, democratic Principles of Government and their example of a free association of independent Indian nations;

(2) the Congress also hereby reaffirms the constitutionally recognized government-to-government relationship with Indian tribes which has historically been the cornerstone of this Nation's official Indian policy;

(3) the Congress specifically acknowledges and reaffirms the trust responsibility and obligation of the United States Government to Indian tribes, including Alaska Natives, for their preservation, protection and enhancement, including the pro vision of health, education, social and economic assistance programs as necessary, to assist tribes to perform their governmental responsibility to provide for the social and economic well-being of their members and to preserve tribal cultural identity and heritage; and

(4) the Congress also acknowledges the need to exercise the utmost good faith in upholding its treaties with the various tribes, as the tribes understood them to be, and the duty of a great Nation to uphold its legal and moral obligations for the benefit of all of its citizens so that they and their posterity may also continue to enjoy the rights they have enshrined in the United States Constitution for time immemorial.

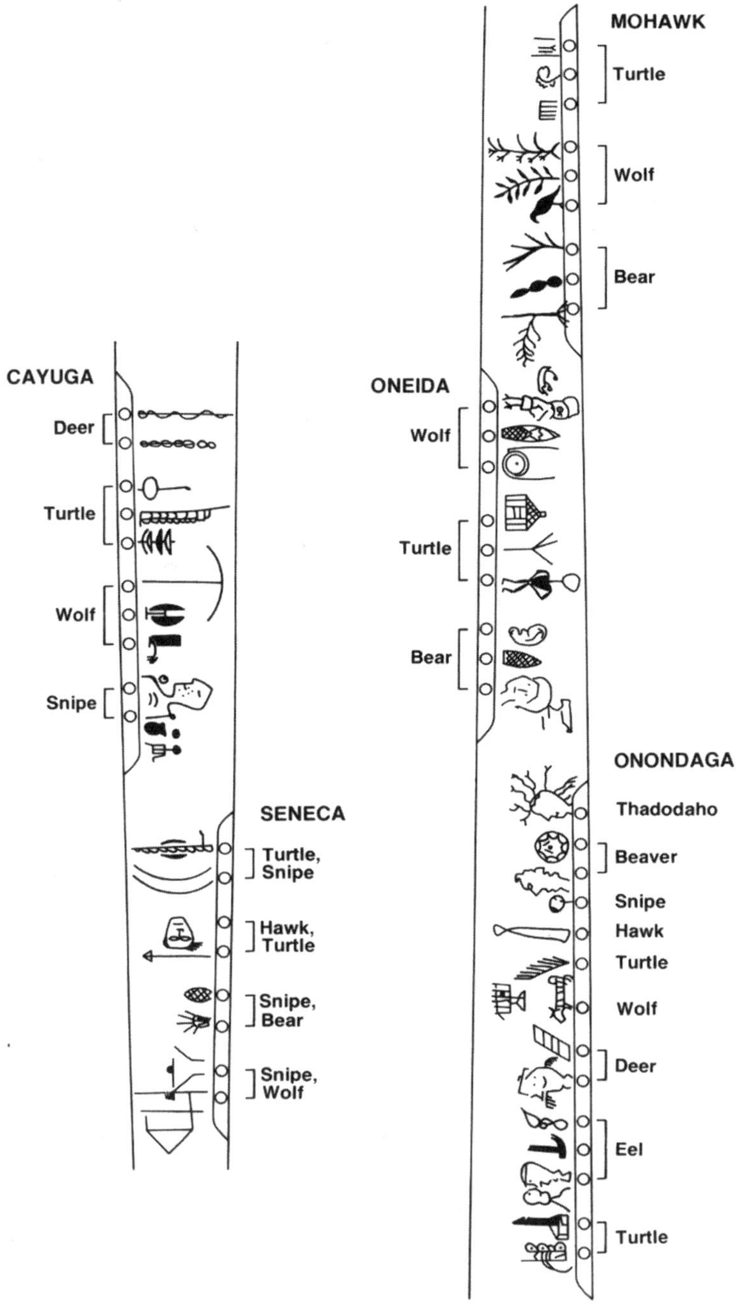

Pictographs of Iroquois Chiefs

Additional Documentary Evidence

by Gregory Schaaf
©1988

Eleven years ago, I was visiting a friend one day, and we were talking about the past and antiques and fine arts, and the telephone rang. It was an acquaintance named Susanna Morgan, whose late husband was the great-great-great-great-grandson of George Morgan, the first Indian agent for the Continental Congress. Nan, as we called her, mentioned to my friend that she had some old family papers and wanted to find an historian to look into them.

A meeting was arranged at which time Nan showed me four letters written to George Morgan by George Washington, Thomas Jefferson, Benedict Arnold, and John Hancock. The document that captured my interest the most was the last, written in April of 1776. The letter directed Morgan to take a great peace belt with thirteen diamonds and 2,500 wampum beads to the confederacy of the western Indian Nations, especially to the Haudenosaunee, the Six Nations, to inspire them with sentiments of justice and hospitality, and to begin the process of negotiating an agreement between those nations.

So I began my search for what happened on Morgan's journey when he traveled across the west to meet with the leaders of the western Indian nations. And I found finally at the Andrew Carnegie Library, part of George Morgan's private diary and letter book. Unfortunately, though, there was a gap for the period from 1776 on. So I kept culling through documents and reels and reels of microfilm, searching.

Every week I'd visit Nan and we'd have a cup of tea and I'd report on my discoveries about the significance of these papers.

Towards the end of one of our meetings, she casually said, "By the way, Gregory, I was up in the attic the other day cleaning some things out and I came across an old chest, and in that chest I found some documents." And she brought out a stack that she could barely lift. She's only 5 ft. tall and less that 100 lbs., and she lifted them with all her strength, laid them on my lap, and said, "Here, maybe these will help answer some of your questions."

Very carefully I untied the knot and unfolded it and began to turn the yellowed pages. I found copies of old Indian treaties. I found documents relating to Benjamin Franklin and Patrick Henry. I found the documents which represent the origins of corporations in America, the original land companies which the Founding Fathers were up to their ears in, involving millions of acres of land and plans for the future of this land. Finally, down towards the bottom, I found the 73 missing pages of Morgan's private journal for the year 1776, which described what happened after John Hancock had given him instructions to establish the first Indian agency for the United States government, and to take this great Peace Belt.

On April 19, 1776, John Hancock and Congress appointed Morgan to be their Indian agent. They told him to provide a great Peace Belt, with 13 diamonds and 2,500 wampum beads, to be delivered to the leaders of the western Indian nations. A duplicate belt was also delivered to the Lenni Lenape or Delaware Nation who are the grandfathers of the Algonquin family of nations.

At that time, the Iroquois and Algonquin peoples and the other Indian nations of this land truly held a balance of power within their hands. If they, at that crucial juncture when America was being born, had joined the British and attacked from the west as the British attacked from the east, the Revolution clearly could have been crushed. These United States of America might not have become as they are today.

I found in the documents that just before the Founding Fathers were about to make their Declaration of Independence, a delegation of the Haudenosaunee came before Congress. They came there to recognize the United States that was about to be born. They were also opening diplomatic relations between the revolutionary government and their own.

John Hancock and the members of the Congress were so impressed by the ideas of democracy as expressed by these chiefs that they addressed them as brothers, because the original relationship between the United States government and the Indian nations was a brother-to-brother relationship, a shoulder-to-shoulder relationship. John Hancock said to the Iroquois ambassadors, "We hope the friendship between us and you will be firm and continue as long as the sun shall shine and the waters run, that we and you may be as one people and have but one heart and be kind to one another like brethren . . ."

When George Morgan, being the Indian agent representing the United States, addressed the Indian nations, he said to them, "Brothers, we are not only inclined to do you justice in all things, but we wish to promote your happiness and to render you every service in our power if you tell us what you want. We therefore desire you to be wise and that your wise people will consider this matter well, for we wish to see you a happy people and to live with you in friendship forever. Speak your minds free when you come to the treaty that we may understand you . . ."

The Onondaga ambassadors gave to John Hancock an Indian name: they called him Karandawan which, roughly translated, means symbol for the American revolutionaries and became the tree of liberty."The Great Tree of Liberty." The Peacemaker inspired the warriors to bury their weapons under the Tree of Peace -- perhaps the oldest historical evidence of an effort for disarmament in the history of the world -- and this tree became a symbol of peace.

Atop that tree is the eagle holding arrows in his talons. The Peacemaker said that each arrow represented a nation. One arrow alone might easily be broken but not so easily if they were bound together. That impressed the Founding Fathers and they took this symbol when they were designing the national emblem.

At the very first Indian-U.S. peace treaty in 1776, there were certain promises that were made to the Indian nations. Our governments promised theirs that we would always respect their land rights. We promised that we would respect their right to justice. We also promised that their young men would never have to fight in our wars unless they volunteered to do so.

These documents proved without a shadow of a doubt that the Haudenosaunee had made a tremendous effort to promote peace between the two sides in the American Revolution. That does not appear in our high school history books. In fact, when the British held a conference at Niagara, George Morgan had one of his spies infiltrate that conference, a spy who was so persuasive that he served as an interpreter between the British Colonel Butler and the Indian nations. At that conference, Butler warned the Haudenosaunee not to trust the Americans. "They plan to deceive you and take all of your lands from you." The Haudenosaunee said, "You say that our brothers who were born on this same continent as us, the Americans, that they plan to cheat us. That may be true, but we are strong enough to defend ourselves. You have told us what a great power you are, that the British have the might and that the king is the father. If you are so strong and mighty, why do you need our help to get involved in this white man's quarrel? If they attack us, we know that they are jealous of our lands and plan to take larger strides, but we are strong enough to stand up against them in the meantime. But they have told us, through our younger brother George Morgan, to sit in peace and to stay out of this war, to think about our children and our grandchildren and our women, that our young men not be killed in this war because it might cause the tears to come down our cheeks."

And so, in 1776, the Haudenosaunee Grand Council called back in all of the warriors. They called them back in to stop their involvement in the war. However, at the same time, George Washington and three of his generals secretly came into Philadelphia at night to lobby Congress to change the policy from one of peace and neutrality to one which would allow him to actively recruit Indian people into the war.

George Morgan was a young man and very idealistic. He thought it was very exciting to be able to participate in the creation of a new nation. So he began visiting with his neighbor, in Philadelphia, the elder statesman Benjamin Franklin, who had created a club to talk about ideas. Franklin had compiled a remarkable record of the meetings that had taken place. And what I found is that there was a long heritage that the Founding Fathers were well aware of that had taken place throughout the colonial period. Morgan traveled from village to village appearing before the Grand Councils and he was particularly impressed by the way in which their governments were conducted.

As I began searching the roots of these documents I had an opportunity about five years ago to speak before the United Nations and since the United Nations stood within the territory which was part Algonquin and part Iroquoian, I decided that I would seek the counsel and advice of the Grand Council of the Haudenosaunee. And so I traced the White Roots of Peace back to Onondaga and I presented them with a copy of these Morgan papers and we began to go through these documents. They told me, "This is what our grandparents and our great-grandparents always said, we just never could prove it. We knew that our ancestors had taken a very strong stand to promote peace and neutrality during the Revolution but we couldn't prove it."

Imagine that you're back 200 years ago, and you really have a chance to create a nation, to form a nation. Where would you search for ideas? Well, it's true that they were looking at the classics, that they were looking at the French philosophers. Where did the French philosophers get their ideas? Many of them came from Jesuit relations documents. Where were they getting their ideas? They were talking to the Haudenosaunce.

The comparison of the Constitution and the Great Law of Peace shows not only the similarities of the three part system of government but also the differences. The fundamental structure of the United

States government -- its system of checks and balances, the separation of powers -- clearly was modeled on the Iroquois Grand Council. The differences also are interesting. The Founding Fathers, for instance, left out of the Constitution the rights of women. The Tadodaho has pointed out to me that within their system he is not a dictator; he can only serve the best interests of the people. It is the women who are the ones who are entrusted with the right to oversee. In addition, one of the qualifications of leadership within the Iroquois society is that, first and foremost, their leaders must be honest in all things.

The Haudenosaunee Grand Council is perhaps the oldest participatory democracy on earth. The principles of this council are still alive, they are still a dynamic document. Our rights as we, the people can be protected only as long as we, the people know what our rights are. In order to know what those rights are we must study the Constitution, search into the principles of the Great Law of Peace. Perhaps that vision of the great prophet who came upon this earth, as the elders say, a thousand years ago, a vision of a world without war, might one day come true. Thank you very much for inviting me.